The Communist Party of China: the Past, Present and Future of Party Building

By Liu Jingbei, et al

Published by
ACA Publishing Ltd.
University House
11-13 Lower Grosvenor Place,
London SW1W 0EX, UK
Tel: +44 (0)20 7834 7676 Fax: +44 (0)20 7973 0076
E-mail: info@alaincharlesasia.com

Web: www.alaincharlesasia.com
Beijing Office
Tel:+86(0)10 8472 1250 Fax:86(0)10 5885 0639
Written by Liu Jingbei
Edited by Martin Savery, ACA Publishing Ltd
Translated by Shi Zhikang
© People's Publishing House, 2015
This translation is published by ACA Publishing Ltd in association with People's Publishing House

ALL RIGHTS RESERVED. NO PART OF THIS
PUBLICATION MAY BE REPRODUCED IN MATERIAL FORM,
BY ANY MEANS, WHETHER GRAPHIC,
ELECTRONIC, MECHANICAL OR OTHER, INCLUDING
PHOTOCOPYING OR INFORMATION STORAGE, IN
WHOLE OR IN PART, AND MAY NOT BE USED TO PREPARE
OTHER PUBLICATIONS WITHOUT WRITTEN
PERMISSION FROM THE PUBLISHER.

The greatest care has been taken to ensure accuracy but the publisher can accept no responsibility for errors or omissions, or for any liability occasioned by relying on its content.
ISBN 978-1-910760-09-3
The Communist Party of China: the Past, Present and Future of Party Building is available from the National Bibliographic Service of the British Library.

Preface

What is the state system of China? How has the Communist Party of China (CPC) managed to exercize long-term governance and to lead the Chinese people from one victory to another? What are the 'secrets' of the CPC's governance? What is China's development road? What significant strategies have been adopted in China? What is the next step in China's development? Why has China been able to achieve such rapid economic development? These are just some of the many questions frequently asked by the international community, especially foreign political parties and statesmen on their visits to China. For the purpose of providing answers to these questions and enabling readers to be informed about the real China and the CPC, we arranged for the *Understanding Modern China* Series (hereinafter referred to as the Series) to be written, to serve as elementary documents introducing the CPC, as well as China's development road, development theories and development experience.

The Series is inspired by the new philosophies, new ideas and new strategies for the country's governance put forward by General Secretary Xi Jinping since the 18th National Congress of the CPC, aimed at the following aspects: strenuously reflecting the development vision of 'the Chinese Dream' and the development prospects of the 'Two Centenary' goals; strenuously reflecting the coordinated promotion of the overall situation of a 'five-pronged approach to building socialism with Chinese characteristics to build up socialist economy, socialist democracy, socialist advanced culture, socialist harmonious society and socialist ecological civilisation; and the strategic arrangements for the 'Four-Pronged Comprehensive Strategy' comprehensively completing the building of a moderately prosperous society in all respects, comprehensively deepening reform in all respects, comprehensively advancing the rule of law, and comprehensively exercising strict discipline for the party; strenuously reflecting the 'new normal' facilitating and leading China's economic development and the implementation of the 'five major development concepts' to promote innovative, coordinated, green, open and shared development; strenuously reflecting the three major economic development strategies of the 'Belt and Road', the coordinated development of Beijing, Tianjin and Hebei province, and the Yangtze river economic belt. On the basis of a great number of fresh cases and experiences, the Series tells China's story, transmits China's voice, analyzes China's problems, and offers China solutions.

The Series has been written on the basis of telling China's story and transmitting China's voice, oriented around the following four aspects: the first is to illustrate the new measures taken to deepen reform since the 18th National Congress of the CPC, the new ideas on economic development and the new philosophy on foreign affairs, on the basis of an all-round introduction to the achievements since the reform and opening up; the second is to analyze the reason for the achievements, the underlying operating law, and the process of evolution, while presenting the development achievements of China's economy and society; the third is to keep to problem orientation and demand orientation, rather than attempt to be all-embracing and systematic, so as to clear up targeted doubts and confusion on the basis of the demands of foreign readers; the fourth is to introduce China not only in terms of 'where it is coming from', but also in terms of 'where it is going', for the purpose of enabling readers to know about China's historical development process on the one hand, and on the other hand, exemplifying and clarifying how China assures the organic unification of its past, present and future, the organic combination of legacy and innovation, and how China is planning its future development.

Under the guidance of the International Department of the CPC Central Committee, the writing of the Series has been organized by China Executive Leadership Academy Pudong (CELAP).

The International Department of the CPC Central Committee is the functional department of the CPC in charge of foreign affairs. So far, the CPC has established connections of various types with more than 600 political parties and organizations in over 160 countries and regions, which include left-wing and right-wing parties; both ruling parties and opposition parties. Foreign affairs work is of paramount importance to the CPC, and an indispensable component of national diplomacy as a whole, whose target is to promote state-to-state and people-to-people communication and understanding.

Preface

CELAP is a national leadership institution in China, and as a platform on which international cooperative training and exchange are carried out, CELAP has held fast to its characteristics of internationality and openness since March 2005 when it was founded. CELAP spares no effort in implementing international cooperative training, with target participants being foreign political parties and statesmen, high-ranking business executives and senior professionals. By the end of 2015, CELAP had offered training programs to more than 6,000 participants from over 130 countries, and thus has won wide recognition and received a favorable reception from the countries, regions and participants that are involved.

To cater for the needs of foreign participants, CELAP initiated the writing of the Series at the beginning of 2012, and after four years of modifications and improvements, the finalized manuscripts were completed at the end of 2015. The first batch of 10 books to be published in this Series are: *China's New Strategies for Governing the Country; The Communist Party of China: the Past, Present and Future of Party Building; China's Reform, Opening Up and Construction of Development Zones; The Framework of the Chinese Government and Public Services; A New Analysis of Urbanization in China; China's Agriculture and Rural Development in the Post-Reform Era; The Evolution of China's Diplomacy in the Modern Era; Leadership Selection and Appointment in China; Leadership Education and Training in China;* and *Shanghai – the 'Pacesetter' of China's Reform and Opening Up.*

The authors of the Series are mainly professionals in CELAP, and functionaries and specialists in the Development Research Center of the Shanghai Municipal People's Government, Shanghai Institute for International Studies and Hangzhou Research Center for Urban Studies.

The Series is published in Chinese and English, with the English translation done mainly by senior professors at Shanghai International Studies University, to whom thanks are due. Gratitude also goes to the People's Publishing House for its great support and positive suggestions in the process of writing and translating.

Writing such a series of textbooks for mature foreign students is a first in China. Constructive criticism is welcome, for the Series as a new endeavor can hardly be free from mistakes.

Editorial Committee of the *Understanding Modern China* Series
January 2016

The Editorial Committee of the Understanding Modern China Series

Directors: Guo Yezhou Feng Jun

Vice Directors: Zhou Zhongfei   An Yuejun

Members: (Listed alphabetically)

An Yuejun	Chen Zhong	Feng Jun
Guo Yezhou	He Lisheng	Jiang Haishan
Li Man	Li Yanhui	Liu Genfa
Liu Jingbei	Wang Guoping	Wang Jinding
Yang Jiemian	Zhao Shiming	Zheng Jinzhou
Zhou Zhenhua	Zhou Zhongfei	

Editor-in-Chief: Feng Jun

Alain Charles Asia (ACA) Publishing Ltd is delighted to be associated with the People's Publishing House to bring this series of 10 *Understanding Modern China* books to an English-speaking readership.

ACA, formerly known as ACP (Alain Charles Publishing) Ltd Beijing, was founded in October 1989 and was the first foreign-owned publishing company to be allowed to open an office in China.

In 2007, ACP Beijing was renamed ACA Publishing Ltd to better reflect its focus on China and the Asia-Pacific region. The company specialises in publishing books about China for international readers and has offices in Beijing and London.

ACA Publishing Ltd,

April 2016

Contents

Introduction XI

1. What Sort of Political Party is the CPC? 1
   I. The CPC is a Party Organised by China's Advanced Elements 2
   II. Marxism as Its Guiding Ideology 5
   III. The Sole Purpose of the CPC is to Serve the People Wholeheartedly ... 8
   IV. The CPC Cares Earnestly about the Party's Work Style 11
   V. The CPC is the Core of Leadership for the Cause of Socialism with Chinese Characteristics 15

2. Why Should China Implement a Multiparty Cooperation System Under the Leadership of the CPC? 21
   I. The Origins of the Multiparty Cooperation System Under the Leadership of the CPC 21
   II. The Implications of the Multiparty Cooperation System Under the Leadership of the CPC 30
   III. Unique Advantages of the Multiparty Cooperation System Under the Leadership of the CPC 35

3. What Does the CPC Depend On For Effective Organization and Cohesion? 38
   I. Rigorous Organizational System 38
   II. Scientific Organizational System 43
   III. Party Building Focused on Ideology 48
   IV. Upholding the Principle that the Party Should Supervise Its Own Conduct and Run Itself with Strict Discipline 51

4. How Does the CPC Govern the Country? 54
   I. Main Governance Experience of the CPC 54
   II. The Historical Position of the CPC 56
   III. The Governing Style of the CPC 58
   IV. Building the CPC's Governance Capability 60

5. How Does the CPC Develop Intra-party Democracy? 67
   I. Ensuring the Democratic Rights of CPC Members 68
   II. Improving the Intra-party Democratic System 73
   III. Enriching Intra-party Democracy Methods 80

6. How Does the CPC Manage Party Members and Allow Them to Play Their Role? 83
   I. Enforcing High Membership Requirements to Ensure High-quality CPC Members 84
   II. Strengthening the Education and Management of CPC Members to Improve their Quality 87
   III. Giving Full Play to the Exemplary and Vanguard Role of CPC Members 89

7. How Does the CPC Combat Corruption and Build a Clean Government? 92
   I. Strengthening Education to Form an Anti-corruption Ideology ...92
   II. Imposing Severe Punishment to Prevent Corruption 96
   III. Improving Relevant Systems to Prevent Corruption 101
   IV. Strengthening Supervision by Establishing an Anti-corruption Safeguard Mechanism 106

8. How Does the CPC Pool the Strength of All Walks of Life for National Development? 112
   I. Stick to Fairness and Justice, and Take a Holistic Approach ...113
   II. Properly Handle Every Type of Social Contradiction 114
   III. Establish and Improve a Mechanism for Coordinating Interests 116
   IV. Consolidate and Develop the Broadest Possible Patriotic United Front 119
   V. Properly Handle Relations with Union, Youth and Women's Organizations 121

9. What is the Relationship between the CPC and China's Military Power 124
   I. Origin of the People's Liberation Army 124

II. The New Military Force 129
　　III. The People's Military Force 132
　　IV. Adhering to the CPC's Absolute Leadership over the Army........137

10. How Does the CPC Handle Its Relations with Other Countries' Political Parties? 143
　　I. The CPC's Principles and Policies for Interparty Relations ..143
　　II. Goals and Objectives of the CPC's Interparty Relations 145
　　III. The Content and Forms of the CPC's Interparty Relations ..147

Chapter Follow-up Questions and References 152

Introduction

I. Teaching Goals

Historically, China has always been an economically prosperous country with a large population and vast territories, creating one of the greatest civilizations that dates back 5,000 years. However, the defeat of the Qing dynasty in the Opium War in 1840 exposed the country to the ambitious expansion of capitalism and imperialism. China therefore suffered from relentless exploitation by nearly every imperialist country since then, while its social structure underwent a major transformation from feudalism to semi-colonialism and semi-feudalism. To free the country from domestic struggle and foreign invasion, many progressive intellectuals strove to find potential remedies. But their tenacious efforts, however unremitting, failed to alleviate the grim fate many Chinese common people tried to escape.

After Russia's October Revolution in 1917, Marxism-Leninism became enormously popular in China, which laid the ideological foundation for the birth of the Communist Party of China (CPC). And China's May Fourth Movement in 1919 provided great opportunities for integrating Marxism with labor movements, a crucial step toward the founding of the CPC. Its official establishment came during July 23-31, 1921 when the first National Congress of the CPC was convened in Shanghai. Since then, the CPC has shed light on both the dim revolutionary path and the once uncertain future.

For more than nine decades, Chinese people have accomplished three remarkable feats under the leadership of the CPC. First, the New Democratic Revolution overthrew feudalism, imperialism and bureaucrat capitalism, and independence was achieved with the founding of the People's Republic of China (PRC). Second, the socialist revolution was started. China finished the socialist transformation of agriculture, capitalist industry and commerce as well as handicraft industry and set up a socialist system. Third, the Reform and Opening-up policy was formulated. China has advanced its socialist modernization drive and further developed and improved socialism with Chinese characteristics. The three major events have changed the historical course of the whole Chinese nation in a fundamental way, which gives China a completely new look.

China's rapid growth has attracted worldwide attention. Especially in recent years, there have been ceaseless discussions about the 'Chinese Economic Miracle', 'Chinese Economic Model' and 'Chinese Economic Experience', where the CPC is constantly referenced. Because none of these achievements would have been possible without the considerable efforts devoted by the CPC. But one may wonder: What is the CPC? Why is it able to unite the Chinese people and register such outstanding achievements? How does the CPC build itself and how can it retain energy and vitality after vicissitudes? Our teaching goal is to discuss and answer these questions.

II. Framework of the Book

This book consists of the following 10 chapters: 1. What is the CPC and what are its structure, guiding ideology, fundamental purpose and work style? In Chapter One, we try to answer these questions in a holistic manner and help readers get a general understanding of the CPC. 2. Every country has its unique party system. So what is China's political party system and why does it fit China? In Chapter Two, we elaborate on the history, connotations and unique advantages of the CPC-led multi-party cooperation system so that readers will better understand the inevitability of the system's success in China. 3. The CPC now has more than 88 million members, a figure that exceeds the population of many big countries. So how can the CPC unite its members and strive to achieve a shared goal? That is what we will discuss in Chapter Three. 4. Chapter Four addresses the experience the CPC has accumulated in its governance over the past 60-odd years as well as the following questions: How does the CPC improve its ruling style and how does it strengthen its governance capacity? 5. The CPC has always maintained that intra-party democracy is vital to its existence. So how does it develop intra-party democracy? Chapter Five introduces how the CPC safeguards the democratic rights of its members, improves intra-party democracy and diversifies methods of democracy. 6. A CPC member is the basic functional unit, which dictates the efficiency of the party. And Chapter Six details how the CPC efficiently manages an extremely large group of members and how it makes sure that party members play an exemplary and vanguard role in their work. 7. Party officials are responsible for managing party affairs and organizing governance activities. So it is a matter of considerable significance for the CPC to ensure that power is not abused. In Chapter Seven, we focus on the party's efforts to combat corruption and build a clean government through education, punishment, regulations and supervision of party members. 8. China has a population of more than 1.3 billion. It still seems a mystery how the CPC rallies and mobilizes other political parties, social groups, all ethnic groups, people from all walks of life as well as Chinese patriots to devote their time and energy to socialist construction and fight for the cause of the great rejuvenation of the Chinese nation. We try to clear up the mystery in Chapter Eight and hope to enlighten readers. 9. Foreign friends with a keen interest in China always wonder: what is the relationship between the CPC and China's military? In Chapter Nine, we give thorough explanations by introducing the origin, nature and leadership of China's military. 10. It is a tradition of the CPC to develop friendly relations with political parties abroad. So when it comes to inter-party communication, what principle does the CPC follow and how does it cope with such relationships? These questions, which many foreign friends show great interest in, are discussed in Chapter Ten. To sum up, we will try to answer the questions mentioned above simply and vividly, in the hope that officials of foreign political parties and governments can gain a basic understanding of the CPC and its governance philosophy and experience.

III. Reading Suggestions

It is almost impossible to understand the theories and practices that have brought the CPC so far without knowing about the theory of Marxism on political parties and the history of the CPC in the larger context of Chinese history since 1840. So we offer the following suggestions: First, get to know Marxist-Leninist theory concerning the establishment of political parties by reading classic works, especially *The Communist Manifesto*; second, familiarize yourself with Chinese history, especially the history of the CPC; and third, find more information about China's basic political system and party system. These steps may give readers an insight into the nature of the CPC and an overview of how the party builds itself. Despite the fact that every country has its specific conditions and unique party system that may have both pros and cons, we hope our readers, particularly foreign party leaders or government officials, tailor the experience the CPC has gained in party-building to their own needs so as to better govern their country and benefit their people.

This book is the fruit of collective wisdom. Scholars, including Liu Jingbei, Wei Shujun, Hao Aili, Tang Canming, Miao Kaijin, Li Wei, Li Peng and Li Jinghua, have made brilliant contributions to the composition of this book. And Liu Jingbei has done an excellent job of compiling and final editing. In this process, leaders from the China Executive Leadership Academy Pudong (CELAP) have given their valuable advice in panel discussions. We are also grateful to its teaching administration department for its strong support. Meanwhile, we also referred to a great number of studies by experts and scholars in this field, many of whom have shown generous support for our work. We would like to express our heartfelt gratitude to all.

Chapter 1

What Sort of Political Party is the CPC?

The Communist Party of China (CPC) is the vanguard both of the Chinese working class and of the Chinese people and the Chinese nation. It is the core of leadership for the cause of socialism with Chinese characteristics and represents the development trend of China's advanced productive forces, the orientation of China's advanced culture and the fundamental interests of the overwhelming majority of the Chinese people. The realization of communism is the highest ideal and ultimate goal of the party. The CPC takes Marxism-Leninism, Mao Zedong Thought, Deng Xiaoping Theory, the important thought of Three Represents and the Scientific Outlook on Development as its guide to action. – Constitution of the Communist Party of China.

No ruling party in any other country is as mysterious as the CPC. Like ancient China, which was a land of wonders and mysteries, the CPC never ceases to attract attention from the outside world. Questions are asked as to what sort of political party it is, why it still keeps its vitality after so many years in power, how it manages to win such wide support and why it plays so significant a role in the development of Chinese society. These are the main topics we are going to discuss in this chapter.

The Flag of the CPC

The 18th National Congress of the CPC, held in Beijing, November 8-14, 2012 (Li Tao, Xinhua News Agency)

I. The CPC is a Party Organised by China's Advanced Elements

In the development history of the world's political parties, many of them have not explicitly defined their nature, while the *Constitution of the CPC* fully and unequivocally prescribes that "the CPC is the vanguard of both the Chinese working class and of the Chinese people",[1] which reveals its advanced nature and class foundation.

1. The Chinese working class lays the foundation for the CPC

According to Marxist political philosophy, a political party is an organization of people from a certain social class, stratum or group that seeks to achieve goals common to its members through the acquisition and exercise of political power. As an active organizer and leader, every political party has a class foundation and represents the will and interest of people in that class. The emergence of bourgeois parties preceded that of working-class parties which occurred as a brainchild of the workers' struggle against the exploitation of capitalists under the guidance of Marxism. The first working-class party in history was the Communist League founded in June 1847 by Karl Marx and Friedrich Engels.

---

[1] *Constitution of the Communist Party of China*, Beijing: People's Publishing House, 2012

The CPC was the inevitable outcome of integrating Marxism-Leninism with China's labor movement. With the Chinese working class at its core, the CPC shows many characteristics peculiar to the group. In the old China, the Chinese working class lacked any means of production, as was the case for the working class elsewhere in the world. But they were closely connected to mass industrial production, representing the most advanced productive forces. In their long struggle against capitalists, they gradually developed into the most advanced, revolutionary and promising social class with an unprecedented level of coordination and strict discipline. In socialist China, the working class – who used to suffer from brutal exploitation and oppression – now commands the means of production, and even leads the country. However, as the bourgeoisie was eradicated from China, the working class, as the representative of advanced productive forces, did not decline in influence but attracted even more well educated fresh blood in the cause of socialist construction, especially since the reform and opening up, and modernization. The changes in its internal structure, living conditions, how and where to work have been helpful in tapping workers' full potential in the long run. So in this new era, with its close connection with modern industrial production, the working class remains not only the representative of the most advanced productive forces and production relations but the most forward-looking, unselfish and disciplined social class that is bound to embrace its new developmental stage over time.

2. Advanced Elements make the CPC

One of the most important principles of Marxist political philosophy is that the communist party must be established by 'advanced elements' of the working class. Marx and Engels pointed out in *The Communist Manifesto* that "the communists are the most advanced and resolute part of the working class of every country, and they push the party forward."[2] This indicates that the CPC is closely connected with, but not equal to, the working class because it is an advanced organization of the working class rather than an ordinary one. To consider the party an ordinary organization or its members an ordinary group of workers would be a denial of its advanced nature. The CPC has since its founding attached great importance to the advanced nature of its members and has rallied to its support a large number of them with communist consciousness, who have also become the vanguard of the Chinese working class.

---

[2] *Constitution of the Communist Party of China,* Beijing: People's Publishing House, 2012

However, this does not mean that non-working-class people are denied entry into the CPC or that taking those people in would change its role as a vanguard of the working class. The social background of a party member is not the decisive factor in granting membership. Any political party, even if the working class does not constitute the majority of its members, can be the vanguard of the class as long as it takes Marxism as its guide, stands firmly with the working class and rules for the fundamental interests of the overwhelming majority of the people. So the CPC still maintains its pure nature as the vanguard of the working class, despite the fact that many party members were born into peasant families in revolutions and wars. Then how can the CPC make non-working-class people ready to join the party and attain vanguard consciousness? Marx and Engels gave their answer: with the development of the labor movement, those from other social classes are allowed to join in on condition that "they allow their actions to be guided by the proletarian world outlook and do not bring with them the remnants of the bourgeoisie and petty bourgeoisie."[3] In the course of democratic revolution and socialist construction, the CPC granted membership to many of those who were not working class, who had replaced their bourgeois world view with a Marxist one and upheld the party's basic line and basic program. Only when they became fully qualified as 'advanced elements' and underwent a period of observation could they be granted full membership.

Some may ask: why does the CPC emphasize its role as the vanguard of the Chinese people and the Chinese nation since it has mentioned its role as the vanguard of the working class and its common practice of transforming a non-working-class person into an 'advanced element' with communist consciousness?

That emphasis exactly demonstrates the CPC's willingness to keep up with the times. While the party highlights its position as the vanguard of the working class, it also realizes that it has to serve the fundamental interests of the Chinese people and the Chinese nation because its power to run the country ultimately comes from the overwhelming majority of Chinese people. Since the introduction of the reform and opening-up policy, the CPC has had to deal with enormous changes in China's social structure: the emergence of various social strata and groups consisting of entrepreneurs and technical personnel employed by private technology enterprises, managerial and technical staff employed by foreign-funded enterprises, the self-employed, private entrepreneurs, employees in intermediaries and

---

[3] *Selected Works of Marx and Engels*, Vol. III, Beijing: People's Publishing House, 1995(2), page 685

New members of the CPC at the site of the First National Congress of the CPC, Shanghai (Cai Weishuai, Xinhua News Agency)

freelance professionals. With the accelerated pace of reform and opening up, and socialist construction, there will be greater social mobility across industries and regions, which means more frequent changes in social identity. Newly prosperous people, most of whom have made their contributions to social progress through hard work and lawful business operations under the guidance and leadership of the CPC, are all builders of socialism with Chinese characteristics. The party should take in advanced elements among those who accept its program and constitution, work hard to conscientiously realize the party's basic line and program, and meet the qualifications of CPC membership after a long test period, in order to increase the influence and rallying force of the party in society at large. Newly joined party members can enhance their political awareness with the help of the CPC. In that sense, the CPC is the vanguard of both the working class and of the Chinese people and the Chinese nation.

II. Marxism as Its Guiding Ideology

It is clearly stated in the constitution that the "Communist Party of China takes Marxism-Leninism, Mao Zedong Thought, Deng Xiaoping Theory, the important thought of Three Represents and the Scientific Outlook on Development as its guide to action,"[4] a principle that has gradually taken shape during its strenuous historical struggle. The CPC has proved its

---

[4] *Constitution of the Communist Party of China,* Beijing: People's Publishing House, 2012

competence in leading the Chinese people onto a suitable and potentially thriving path of development despite all the setbacks since its birth. What underlines this incredible success is that the party has been adhering to scientific theories, which have proven to precede and guide the reasonable actions of a political party. It is the successful application of Marxism in China and the party's effort to keep up with the times that have enabled it to stand the test of time.

1. Advanced Elements in China accepted Marxism

Some may ask: why did the Chinese people choose Marxism among various theories intended to guide social transformation and development? The answer can be found in the intense suffering of China in modern history.

It is well known that, since the Opium War in 1840, China began its transformation from a feudal society into a semi-colonial and semi-feudal society, reaching its nadir followed by endless suffering and humiliation before 1949. To save the country from the oppression of imperialism and feudalism, the Chinese people had to fight their way through pitch darkness. Though many political factions once threw light on which path the Chinese nation should take, the influence of their political propositions was only transient. One example is the Xinhai Revolution led by Dr Sun Yat-sen in 1911. By overthrowing the Qing dynasty, China's last imperial dynasty, the revolution did put an end to the imperial hegemony that had plagued China for more than 2,000 years and the Republic of China was founded, but China was still a semi-colonial and semi-feudal country, and the presence of imperialism was no less strong due to the tenacious obstruction of diehards, with whom a final compromise was made. No wonder Dr Sun said: "People these days suffer terribly from political corruption and social degeneration that are even more appalling than before the downfall of the Qing dynasty."[5]

So what was the remedy for a country in such a critical situation? It was already evident that the feudal Qing dynasty was unable to withstand a single blow in the war waged by the west. A bourgeois republic also proved impracticable. Multiparty and parliamentary systems were nothing but instruments which warlords, bureaucrats and politicians used to seize power. All these setbacks forced patriots to find new solutions. Before the October Revolution broke out, a large number of new theories were imported to China, including Marxism that quickly attracted the attention of some far-sighted intellectuals. The success of the October Revolution turned the theory

---

[5] *Li Wenhai, Wen Yuequn: The Choice of History, the Choice of the People, People's Daily, June 7, 2001(9)*

into reality. It was so inspiring that Chinese intellectuals gradually arrived at the following consensus: the success of the October Revolution was thanks to the guidance of Marxism; Russia's national reality was similar to China's and the two countries were geographically close to each other, so they could share a similar future. Therefore, these advanced elements sought to learn from Russia and from then on, they shifted their focus from the west to the east, and from bourgeois democracy to socialism. That was how the Chinese people chose Marxism, whose application in China's labor movement gave birth to the CPC.

2. The CPC unswervingly follows and develops Marxism

Created from the integration of the Chinese labor movement and Marxism, the CPC since its birth has taken Marxism as its guide. And in its arduous struggle, the party has integrated the basic tenets of Marxism with the concrete realities of China's revolution and succeeded in finding a development path with distinct Chinese characteristics.

Some may ask: why does Marxism originating in the west have such a great influence on a country so far away? Marx once said that, "whether a theory can be turned into reality in a country depends on how much it satisfies the needs of the country."[6] There are two reasons why Marxism could be successfully applied to revolution, development and reform by all Chinese ethnic groups under the leadership of the CPC. On the one hand, the basic tenets of Marxism comprise incontrovertible truth that has been developed through their application in solving newly emerging problems in new ages, directing labor movements in many countries and vying with other misleading theories. On the other hand, the Chinese communists never consider Marxism an empty or rigid dogma, but rather a theory that must be developed and enriched through practice. They have creatively integrated the basic tenets of Marxism with the concrete reality of the Chinese revolution. Chairman Mao once made a similar statement: "The reason why Marxism was useful in China was that it met China's needs, and that it happened to be correlated with the Chinese revolution and mastered by Chinese people."[7]

In the historical course of Marxist localization in China over 90 years, the CPC has worked out two important theoretical systems. One is Mao Zedong Thought. It is the outcome of the creative application and development of Marxism-Leninism in China and answers the questions of how to carry out

---
[6] *Selected Works of Marx and Engels*, Vol, I, Beijing: People's Publishing House, 1995(2), page 11
[7] *Selected Works of Mao Zedong*, Vol. IV, Beijing: People's Publishing House, 1991(2), page 1,515

the new democratic revolution and socialist revolution in a semi-colonial and semi-feudal country such as China, what kind of socialism should be established and how to achieve that goal, thus enriching Marxism. The other is the theoretical system of socialism with Chinese characteristics that includes Deng Xiaoping Theory, the important thinking of Three Represents and the Scientific Outlook on Development. For a huge country with a population of more than 1.3 billion, it provides detailed answers to what kind of socialism should be established and how to establish it, what kind of party should be built and how to build it as well as how to develop the economy and in what way. The theoretical system of socialism with Chinese characteristics was engendered by Mao Zedong Thought and further develops it.

The development of practice, understanding of the truth, and innovation of theories knows no boundaries. The practice of the party and the people keeps progressing and so should the theories guiding it. Under new historical conditions, the CPC should in a timely manner conduct a thorough review of the new experience our people have accumulated, promptly address new issues emerging in practice, and continuously review new theories, thus providing scientific guidance for practice and ensuring the vitality of scientific theories.

To sum up, the localization of Marxism is a progressive process. The best example is the theoretical system of socialism with Chinese characteristics that has evolved gradually and been enriched by socialist construction with Chinese characteristics. Although Marxism was created in the 1840s, it still plays a significant role in China today. The ability to keep up with the times may help explain its long-lasting popularity. Generations of Chinese communists have made concerted efforts to apply the basic tenets of Marxism to the Chinese revolution, social construction and reform, and made theoretical innovations that further develop the localization of Marxism.

III. The Sole Purpose of the CPC is to Serve the People Wholeheartedly

It seems perplexing to some foreign friends that the CPC has been ruling the country for more than 60 years and winning widespread support. The reason behind it is that the sole purpose of the CPC is to serve the people wholeheartedly.

1. The CPC has no special interests of its own

According to Marxism, "a political party represents the interests of a certain social class". In other words, a political party in a general sense speaks for a certain group of people and acts on their behalf. So the CPC as a political organization of the Chinese working class naturally represents their interests and also the interests of the overwhelming majority of Chinese people. However, the CPC differs from many other political parties in that it clearly states in its constitution that: "The party has no special interests of its own apart from the interests of the working class and the broad masses of the people."[8]

So why does the CPC make that statement? For one thing, it is because the CPC follows the Marxist principles of what makes a proletarian political party. Marx and Engels once pointed out: "All previous historical movements were movements of minorities, or in the interests of minorities. The proletarian movement is the self-conscious, independent movement of the vast majority or in the interests of the vast majority."[9] Thus, they asserted that "the interests of communists are no different from those of the proletariat."[10] From that perspective, a proletarian party does not have special interests of its own, neither does the CPC. For another, it is because of the CPC's representativeness. According to its constitution, the CPC is the vanguard both of the Chinese working class and of the Chinese people and the Chinese nation. It represents the development trend of China's advanced productive forces, the orientation of China's advanced culture and the fundamental interests of the overwhelming majority of its people. Obviously the CPC represents more than any other political parties in the world. It does not speak for any interest group but the Chinese people of all ethnic groups, which means the party is not supposed to have special interests of its own; otherwise it cannot represent the common interests of all ethnic groups. Finally, it is because the CPC continues its honorable practices from the past. The history of the CPC is about self-sacrifice and fighting for the people. In time of democratic revolution, to secure national independence and save the Chinese people from deep water, numerous communists showed indomitable spirit and never displayed the slightest hint of fear either in matters of life and death or in battles of blood and fire. From the recent history of the PRC, we can also find many CPC members working flat out to serve their country: Jiao Yulu, an ordinary civil servant who devoted himself to fighting against economic backwardness despite severe illness; Kong Fansen, a model of industriousness, who worked tirelessly to promote regional development; Zheng Peimin, a self-disciplined party cadre who made great contributions

---

[8] *Constitution of the Communist Party of China,* Beijing: People's Publishing House, 2012
[9] *Selected Works of Marx and Engels,* Vol. I, Beijing: People's Publishing House, 1995(2), page 283
[10] *Selected Works of Marx and Engels,* Vol. I, Beijing: People's Publishing House, 1995(2), page 284

to improve local people's lives in Hunan province and Yang Shanzhou, an ordinary prefectural party committee secretary, devoting his whole frugal life to fulfilling his duties for the benefit of others. It is estimated that, among all the role models from all walks of life, more than 85% of them are members of the CPC. They are the most outstanding part of the party and with what they have done, they provide vivid examples to illustrate that "the CPC has no special interests of its own".

2. The CPC considers serving the people wholeheartedly as its sole purpose

As a political party 'without special interests of its own', the CPC naturally puts the principle of serving the people at the heart of party building. On September 8, 1944, Chairman Mao made the famous speech *Serving the People* in memory of Zhang Side, an ordinary soldier. He said: "The CPC and the Eighth Route Army and New Fourth Army led by the party are battalions of the revolution – totally dedicated to the liberation of the Chinese people and working entirely in people's interests."[11] At the CPC's seventh National Party Congress, he clearly pointed out that "the CPC works for the benefit of the Chinese nation and the Chinese people without seeking special interests of its own. And its members should serve the people rather than transcend them." He also mentioned that "we should serve the masses wholeheartedly and never for a moment should we become divorced from them; we should put the interests of our people first rather than personal or factional interests; there should be a consistency between responsibility to the people and responsibility to the party's leading bodies; these are where our work starts."[12] Since then, the CPC has clarified its founding purpose, and won the wholehearted support of the Chinese people by making enormous efforts to achieve that purpose.

Then how will the CPC fulfill that purpose in the new historical conditions? First, CPC members should strictly follow the regulations in the constitution. The second chapter in the *Constitution of the CPC* prescribes that "members of the CPC are at all times ordinary members of the working people. CPC members must not seek any personal gain or privileges, except for personal benefits and job-related functions and powers prescribed by relevant laws and policies."[13] What needs clarifying is that the party as a political organization is not allowed to seek special interests of its own, but this does not mean that party members cannot seek their personal legitimate

---

[11] *Selected Works of Mao Zedong*, Vol. III, Beijing: People's Publishing House, 1991(2), page 1,004
[12] *Selected Works of Mao Zedong*, Vol. III, Beijing: People's Publishing House, 1991(2), page 1,094
[13] *Constitution of the Communist Party of China,* Beijing: People's Publishing House, 2012

interests. However, their interests are limited by laws and regulations. Pursuit of personal interests beyond legitimate bounds or even placing personal interests above those of the masses are strictly forbidden according to party discipline. Second, corrupt practices must be eradicated. The CPC has always valued the importance of building a clean party. Nowadays, the party faces complicated and severe long-term tests in exercising governance, carrying out reform and opening up, developing the market economy as well as tests from the external environment. And meanwhile, the whole party is confronted with increasingly grave dangers such as lack of drive and competence, being divorced from the masses, corruption and other misconduct. Under such circumstances, some party members are likely to be corrupt. To raise anti-corruption awareness, the party issued a stern warning at the 18th National Congress of the CPC: "If the CPC fails to handle this issue well, it could prove fatal to the party, and even cause the collapse of the party and the fall of the state."[14] There has never been ambiguity in the way the CPC deals with those who undermine the cause of the party and the Chinese people. Once violation of party discipline is identified, there is zero tolerance. Recent cases involving Bo Xilai, former member of the Political Bureau of the CPC Central Committee and Liu Zhijun, former Minister of Railways clearly illustrate that. A 'zero tolerance' policy has proved to be the most effective way of guaranteeing the fundamental interests of the Chinese people. Third, the party should stick to the mass line in its work, doing everything for the masses, relying on them in every task, carrying out the principle of "from the masses, to the masses", and translating its correct views into action by the masses of their own accord. The CPC should take practice as its lifeline and basic roadmap. It has been proved that correct programs, lines and policies would not be formulated without the participation and suggestions of the masses. Only in this way can the party represent their interests. With the party's proper organization and publicity as well as its vanguard role, these top-down directions can in turn help the masses recognize their vital interests and get organized to strive for them.

IV. The CPC Cares Earnestly about the Party's Work Style

The CPC is unique compared with other ruling parties in the world. This uniqueness lies not only in its commitment to Marxism, and its purpose, but also in its incessant efforts to strengthen and rectify the party's work style during the long-term struggle, which distinguishes it from other political parties.

---

[14] Hu Jintao. *Firmly March on the Path of Socialism with Chinese Characteristics and Strive to Complete the Building of a Moderately Prosperous Society in All Respects,* November 8, 2012

1. The CPC has cultivated its fine work style during protracted revolutionary wars

The nature, program and purpose of a political party can be reflected by the consistent attitude and behavior of itself and of its members. This consistent attitude and behavior is called the work style of a political party. During its protracted struggle, the CPC has formed its own fine work style, namely, taking 'integrating theory with practice, maintaining close ties with the masses and practicing criticism and self-criticism' as its essence.

'Integrating theory with practice' has helped the CPC maintain strong creativity. That work style means combining Marxism-Leninism with the concrete reality of the Chinese revolution and construction. To seek truth from facts, we must proceed from reality in all things, which is the work style that we consistently stick to. 'Integrating theory with practice' is the living soul of Marxism, the essence of the ideological line of the CPC, and the key to maintaining the vitality and creativity of the CPC. To truly combine Marxism-Leninism with the concrete situation in China, there are three principles to follow: first, to believe in the universal truth of Marxism, and take it as the scientific guidance for actions; second, to learn from but not copy the successful experience of other countries or parties based on the specific national reality; third, to uphold Marxism and develop it rather than think of it as rigid dogma. From the long-term struggle of the CPC, we can see that sticking to these three principles, we will win continuous victories; departing from them, failure and frustration will ensue. From the New Democratic Revolution to the successful exploration of the socialist road with Chinese characteristics, every historic leap and every bit of progress the party has made have been the result of integrating theory with practice.

'Maintaining close ties with the masses' is the work style that maintains the party's strong combat effectiveness. It means 'doing everything for the masses', relying on them in every task, carrying out the principle of 'from the masses, to the masses', and translating the party's correct views into spontaneous action by the masses. This is another significant trait of the CPC which distinguishes it from other parties. The 'mass line' also can ensure the party's victory in every battle. During the period of revolutionary wars, the CPC upheld the idea of 'people's war', which meant uniting people to fight against powerful enemies at home and abroad, and won the victory of national independence and liberation. The oppressed people finally stood up and became the masters of China. During the socialist construction, the CPC adhered to the guidance of 'mobilizing all positive factors', fully relying on the wisdom and strength of the people and achieving great accomplishments of socialist construction in poverty-stricken China. Since the reform and opening up, the CPC has summed up the experience created by the people and developed principles and policies that reflect the needs and interests of the people, thus making tremendous achievements attracting worldwide attention. The history of the CPC since its birth is the history of maintaining and fighting for people's interests, and of relying on the people to win continuous victories. Comrade Deng Xiaoping pointed out that "any party organization that deplorably loses touch with the masses and does not mend its ways forfeits the source of its strength and will invariably fail and be rejected by the people".[15] Only by trusting and relying on the people can the CPC remove every obstacle and advance from victory to victory.

'Practicing criticism and self-criticism' has helped the CPC to keep a harmonious relationship within the party. So-called criticism and self-criticism, according to the principles and requirements of the party, consist of openly stating the shortcomings and mistakes of others and also conducting strict analysis of oneself. This is another characteristic of the CPC, a way of resolving contradictions within the party, and a forceful weapon to rectify wrong thinking and unhealthy tendencies within the CPC. In every historical period, the party can actively carry out criticism and self-criticism based on changing situations and tasks, as well as major problems within the party, so as to prevent the harm brought by these wrong tendencies. In the early years of democratic revolution, the CPC used this powerful weapon to promptly correct the erroneous line of rightist capitulationism and leftist adventurism. During the Yan'an Rectification Movement, the CPC carried out a policy of 'learning from past mistakes to avoid future ones, curing the illness to save the patient'. By thoroughly practicing criticism and self-criticism, the party has corrected subjectivism, sectarianism, stereotyping and other bad tendencies within the CPC. Shortly after the Third Plenary Session of the Eleventh CPC Central Committee, a nationwide debate about whether practice was the sole criterion for testing truth was carried out and this debate smashed the argument of the 'two whatevers', once again upheld the ideological principle of seeking truth from facts and brought order out of chaos from the Cultural Revolution. The party began to take economic development as the central task. This serious attitude of criticism and self-criticism has helped the party to remain sober-minded, encouraged the party to face and correct its own

---

[15] *The Selected Works of Deng Xiaoping*. Vol II, Beijing, People's Publishing House, 1993, page 42

shortcomings, and eliminated elements that may adversely affect the party's healthy development. This enables the party to move forward in a more mature manner.

In addition, during the long-term practice of revolution, construction and reform, the CPC has also formed a work style of hard work, diligence and frugality, modesty and prudence as well as guarding against arrogance and rashness. That is the valuable experience derived from its arduous struggle, and also the reason why the CPC has been able to become stronger after experiencing innumerable obstacles and difficulties.

2. The CPC will never abandon its fine work style

A series of fine work styles with the above three as the core, have been inherited and developed by generations of CPC members, and have become an essential part of the CPC's ability to maintain the party's advanced nature, purity and high rate of support, and to improve its ability to govern. History and reality have proved that, if a ruling party does not pay attention to building its work style, allowing unhealthy tendencies to erode the party, then it will lose the support of its members as well as that of the people, and may eventually lose power or face the collapse of the party and the country. That's why the CPC will never abandon its fine work style.

In recent years, along with the profound changes in the economic system, social structure, interest patterns and people's ideology, the independence, selectivity, variability and divergence of people's thoughts and activities have strengthened incessantly, and social public opinion has become multilayered, multicategory and diversified. Especially in an era of social change, some CPC members have been unable to deal correctly with conflicts between old ideas and values, and new ones. There has been confusion in thought and behavioral deviation leading to a crisis of faith, lack of trust, moral decline, spiritual emptiness and value distortion. Therefore, the party made it clear in its report to the 18th National Congress of the CPC that "we should carry out intensive activities throughout the party to study and practice its mass line, with the focus on the need to serve the people and to be down-to-earth, honest and upright in conduct"; and "we should always work hard and be frugal. We should make determined efforts to improve the style of writing and meetings, and reject undesirable practices such as mediocrity, laziness, laxity and extravagance, the practice of just going through the formalities, and bureaucratism."[16] Since the First Plenary Session of the 18th Central Committee of the CPC, Comrade Xi Jinping has repeatedly stressed that officials should strictly practice self-discipline to build a clean government. We should also make great efforts to solve problems within the party, such as corruption and being out of touch with the people. We should improve our work style, maintain close ties with the people, be of one mind with them, and share a common destiny with them.

V. The CPC is the Core of Leadership for the Cause of Socialism with Chinese Characteristics

The Constitution of the CPC clearly states that: The CPC is the core of leadership for the cause of socialism with Chinese characteristics. This position of the CPC is not declared by itself, but chosen by the people, by history and by development.

1. The leadership position of the CPC has been established during protracted revolution and construction

The recent history of China demonstrates that neither revolutionary pioneers, nor other political parties or factions found the right path to national independence and people's liberation. After the Opium War in 1840, the Chinese people tried various ways, including the Taiping Rebellion, Hundred Days' Reform and Boxer Rebellion, to get rid of the shackles of exploitation and depression but they all failed. The Xinhai Revolution, led by Dr Sun Yat-sen, overthrew the Qing Dynasty and established the Republic of China, but it did not change China's social system. Only the CPC pointed out the right path to the Chinese people and led them to fight for national independence. After 28 years of arduous struggle, under the guidance of the CPC, the Chinese people won the New Democratic Revolution by establishing the PRC.

After the founding of the PRC, the CPC, as the ruling party, helped transform the nation from a new democratic one into a socialist one, revive the war-ravaged economy, consolidate the people's government, finish the socialist transformation and establish a socialist system. Later, the CPC guided the Chinese people to carry out large-scale socialist construction. During this period, though we took some wrong directions

---

[16] Hu Jintao, *Firmly March on the Path of Socialism with Chinese Characteristics and Strive to Complete the Building of a Moderately Prosperous Society in All Respects – Report at the 18th NPC*, Beijing: People's Publishing House, 2012

and made some mistakes, the whole nation was united and overcame these setbacks. Since the Third Plenary Session of the 11th CPC Central Committee held in 1978, China has entered a new phase of development, and profound changes have also taken place in all aspects: great leaps have been made in the pace of development, the living standard of our people and the comprehensive national power.

Overall, the leadership position of the CPC is determined by its nature as the vanguard of the working class, and has been formed during a protracted period of struggle. In China, no other political organization can attract so many excellent people, have such a well organized system, and keep such a close relationship with the people. It is also the party that has sacrificed the most fighting for the independence of our nation. China's recent history proves that: only under the leadership of the CPC can the Chinese people win national independence and liberation, forge ahead on a socialist road with Chinese characteristics, rejuvenate the country and make it more prosperous. Without the CPC, remarkable achievements such as creating the new China would have been impossible.

2. Socialist modernization must uphold the leadership of the CPC

To uphold the leadership of the CPC is the inherent requirement and guarantee for successfully building socialism with Chinese characteristics. First, it can lead us in the right direction during the drive toward socialist modernization, which must be closely related to the basic socialist system. During the socialist modernization, our goal is to develop China into a prosperous, democratic, civilized and harmonious socialist nation and to realize our Chinese Dream of national rejuvenation, thus fully reflecting the superiority of the socialist system. During this process, only by adhering to the leadership of the CPC, can China forge ahead in the right direction.

Second, only by upholding the leadership of the CPC, can we mobilize more people to join in the drive for reform and socialist modernization. On the one hand, reform and modernization are everyone's responsibility, and we must mobilize them to join this great cause, fully mobilize their wisdom and get their strongest support. The CPC can effectively mobilize the people because it has always been with them. On the other hand, reform is a large-scale social change and a profound and extensive revolution. There is no successful experience to hand for our reference, nor can we simply copy the western model. The problems it faces are extremely complicated, especially in

China, a big country with a large population. Facing such a pressing situation, it needs a strong leadership as the designer and leader of its reform, who can unite and coordinate powers from all groups and lead the reform to success. This core of leadership is the party.

Third, only by upholding the leadership of the CPC, can China maintain long-term stability. It is difficult to carry out modernization smoothly amid political instability, social unrest and low morale. In modern China, the CPC is the only party that can unite the people of all nationalities and maintain the long-term stability of the country.

At present, a small minority of people doubt or deny the leadership of the CPC on the pretext of mistakes the CPC made in the past. This is completely wrong. The CPC has indeed made mistakes, including the Cultural Revolution which caused serious disturbances throughout the country. But we must realize that any party or individual can make mistakes, and sometimes it is inevitable, especially in this case, because the CPC is engaged in an unprecedented cause which has not been undertaken by any other country. The CPC can face up to and learn from its mistakes, and correct them through practice by relying on the power of the people, which is a significant trait that distinguishes it from other political parties. It is obviously wrong to lose faith in the party, or to doubt or deny the leadership of the party just because of mistakes it made in the past.

3. To uphold the leadership of the CPC, we must make party building more scientific in all aspects

Since the early stage of reform and opening up, the CPC has profoundly reviewed the experience of the Chinese revolution and construction, and proactively adjusted its governance functions to suit the changing situation. The CPC, to achieve the strategic goal of writing a new chapter in party building and socialist construction, has proposed that "to uphold the party's leadership, it is imperative to improve that leadership."[17]

To improve the leadership of the CPC, we should continue to make the party's leadership more scientific and bring party building more in line with objective laws. *The Decision of the CPC Central Committee on Major Issues on Strengthening and Improving Party Building under the New Circumstances* passed at the Fourth Plenary Session of the 17th CPC Central Committee explicitly addressed the major issue and task of "making party building more

---

[17] *Selected Works of Deng Xiaoping*: Vol. II, Beijing: People's Publishing House, 1994, page 271

scientific in all aspects". Comrade Xi Jinping gave a comprehensive and insightful explanation of this task, and said that "to make party building more scientific, the CPC should ultimately have a good understanding of, and willingly apply, the rules of building a Marxist ruling party, study new situations, solve new problems and draw on new experience. We will continuously register new achievements in guiding party building with scientific theories, safeguarding party building with scientific systems, and improving party building in scientific ways."[18]

To guide party building with scientific theories, it is crucial to guide party building with theories achieved by integrating Marxism with China's conditions, to try to explore new requirements of party building in promoting scientific development and social harmony, to earnestly sum up experience in strengthening the party's governance capacity and its advanced nature, and to constantly register theoretical innovations in party building.

To safeguard party building with scientific systems, the key is to strictly obey the building laws of a ruling party in system building and to constantly make the systems for party work and party building more integral and scientific. There should be systems for work as well as for procedures. The systems should specify not only the regulations but also how to deal with those who violate the regulations, thus reducing the possibility of discretionary decisions and promoting party building in more scientific, systematic and regulated ways.

To improve party building in a scientific way, it is fundamental to not only inherit and enrich the CPC's experience of successfully boosting party building learnt during long-term practice, but also to actively explore and apply modern scientific techniques, including information technology, modern management, organization and psychology. The CPC should also learn from the good practice of foreign ruling parties in party building, and constantly bolster its work in party building.

The report delivered at the 18th National Congress of the CPC specified the requirements and tasks for "making party building more scientific under new circumstances" which was later included in the *Constitution of the CPC*. Since then, Comrade Xi Jinping has reiterated in a series of speeches these

---

[18] Xi Jinping. *Programmatic Documents on Strengthening and Improving Party Building Under the New Situation. Guidance on the 'Decision' of the Fourth Plenary Session of the 17th CPC Central Committee*, Beijing: Party Building Books Publishing House, 2009, pages 45-46

requirements and tasks stipulated in the report to the 18th National Congress of the CPC, and has required that all CPC members thoroughly understand and earnestly fulfill these requirements and tasks.

Why should the CPC emphasize that party building must be made more scientific? Comrade Xi Jinping has stressed that this requirement is to learn and spread the knowledge of our party's work in maintaining and developing the advanced nature of a Marxist ruling party during a period spanning more than 90 years, and to adapt to and tackle new changes in international, national and CPC situations arising under new circumstances. Over the years, we have advanced the great new undertaking of party building in all aspects, and are continuously making party building more scientific. Meanwhile, there is quite a gap between the CPC's leadership and governance capacity, party building and the abilities and work style of CPC cadres and their capability to withstand changes in domestic and foreign situations or of fulfilling the historic task the CPC is undertaking. In other words, that is why party building should be more scientific. Especially under the new circumstances, the CPC faces long-term, complex and tough challenges in governance, reform and opening up, in the market economy and external environment. Therefore the CPC is more likely to confront growing risks, including lack of drive, incompetence, being divorced from the masses and succumbing to corruption. Thus, it is a major issue to cement the CPC's status and fulfill its obligations as a ruling party by way of making party building more scientific.

How to comprehensively make party building more scientific? To this end, five requirements need to be fulfilled, namely: firmly adhering to the main line of strengthening the party's governance capacity, advanced nature and purity; sticking to the principle of emancipating the mind, reform and innovation; supervising its own conduct and enforcing strict party discipline; comprehensively strengthening the CPC's ideological construction, organizational capacity, style of work, resistance against corruption, and systems; enhancing CPC members' capability for self-purification, self-improvement and self-innovation; and building a Marxist ruling party featuring continuous learning, provision of service and innovation. Our party should give prominence to six aspects of the major tasks proposed at the 18th National Congress of the CPC: to stand firm with their faith in communism; to further enhance the CPC's contacts with the masses; to further expand intraparty democracy; to further consolidate the organizational foundation for the CPC's governance; to rigorously implement the system of accountability for improving party conduct and upholding integrity; and to further enforce strict party discipline. Moreover, there is an urgent need to establish and develop systems that safeguard CPC governance in scientific, democratic and law-based ways, as well as to address prominent contradictions and problems within the party. We should stick to the decisions made at the Third Plenary Session of the 18th National Congress of the CPC, including intensifying the system reform of party building by enhancing the party's scientific, democratic and law-based governance, strengthening the building of democratic centralism, and improving the leadership structure and governing style of the CPC. We should maintain the party's advanced nature and purity, thus providing strong political support for reform and opening up, and socialist modernization.

Chapter 2

Why Should China Implement a Multiparty Cooperation System Under the Leadership of the CPC?

Throughout the world, almost all countries, including developing countries, practice a two-party or multiparty system, except for a handful of countries that have no political parties or practice a single-party system. The Chinese political party system is different from these two-party, multiparty or one-party systems. It is a multiparty cooperation system under the leadership of the CPC. Some may raise questions such as: Why should China implement such a political system? How did it come into being? What is it? What are its features and advantages? In this chapter, we will provide answers to these questions.

I. The Origins of the Multiparty Cooperation System Under the Leadership of the CPC

During years of fighting for national survival and independence, Chinese political parties explored suitable political party systems for over half a century. From the establishment of the Tongmenghui (known in English as the Chinese United League or United Allegiance Society) in 1905, China's first bourgeois political party, until the founding of a multiparty cooperation and political consultative system under the leadership of the CPC, this half century witnessed several different party political models, including the multiparty system, the two-party system and one-party dictatorship. They finally found that the multiparty cooperation system under the leadership of the CPC was the political party system that best suits the national conditions, represents the interests of the general public and meets the needs of China's modernization.

1. The failure of the Multiparty System

The multiparty system failed twice in China. The first attempt failed during the early days of Yuan Shikai's governance and the ensuing Northern Warlord Government. In 1912, after the Republic of China was established, Sun Yat-sen, the Chinese democratic revolution forerunner, took charge of formulating and promulgating *The Provisional Constitution of the Republic of China* before resigning as interim president to uphold democracy and the republic as well as putting strains on his successor Yuan Shikai, an old bureaucratic official.

The Provisional Constitution of the Republic of China, which took after the multiparty system of France, stipulated that the Republic of China practice the accountable cabinet system and bicameral system, with the president coming from the party that wins the majority of seats in parliament, and vesting the senate with the crucial power to review the actions of the president.

During the first congressional election in 1912, the pattern of three factions and four major political parties was formed, namely the Kuomintang (KMT) led by revolutionists, the Democratic Party led by constitutionalists, and the Republic Party and the United Party, which both supported the rule of Yuan Shikai. The KMT became the largest party in the House and Senate (securing 45.4% of the seats), and was given the right to form a cabinet.

However, in order to restore a feudal autocratic system and warlord governance, Yuan Shikai gave the order to assassinate Song Jiaoren, the leader of the KMT and the presidential candidate of the Republic of China. Later, he caused the KMT to disintegrate through various means including buying people off. The Progressive Party and the Civic Party had become his political thugs. The congressional election was totally manipulated by him, and then, after assuming the post of president, he declared the dissolution of the congress and abolished the constitution in January 1914.

Then the bourgeois parliamentary political system copied from the west collapsed. Although some northern warlords, including Duan Qirui, Li Yuanhong, and Cao Kun, later restored the congress, the congress became only a guise for their military dictatorship. Political parties in parliament became ornaments, and the MPs became "greedy pigs" who could be bought off easily, and the multiparty system went completely the wrong way. The reasons for the failure were numerous, of which the most important was that, in a semi-colonial and semi-feudal society, the bourgeois political parties were too weak to fight against the feudal autocratic system and feudal warlords, and parliamentary democracy did not get the support from various social classes, the people, nor did it have any cultural basis. Therefore, there were no real political parties for the multiparty system in the early years of the Republic of China, and all political parties and the parliament were merely puppets under the control of Yuan Shikai and northern warlords.[19]

Table I. Some political parties established in the early years of the Republic of China

Time of Foundation	Name	Representatives
October 1911 to January 1912	The Republic Construction Group	Tang Hualong, Liang Qichao
	The Republic Union Party	Wu Tingfang, Chen Qimei, Yu Youren
	The Chinese Society Party	Jiang Kanghu, Zhang Kegong
	The State Affairs Party	Wang Zhaoming, Yang Du
	The Union of the Republic of China	Hu Yang, Zhang Binglin
	The Republic Construction Party	Ding Rong, Tao Chengzhang, Xiong Xiling
January to August 1912	The United Party	Zhang Binglin, Zhang Jian, Cheng Dequan
	The Republic Party	Li Yuanhong, Zhang Binglin, Liang Qichao
	Republic Radical Party	Li Yuanhong, Huang Xing
	The Federation of the Republic of China	Zhang Binglin, Cheng Dequan, Zhao Fengchang
	Democratic and Socialist Party	Li Yuanhong, Tan Yankai
	The National Association	Wen Zongyao, Wu Guangjian
	The Liberal Party	Li Huaishuang, Dai Chuanxian
August 1912 to February 1913	The KMT	Sun Yat-sen, Huang Xing, Song Jiaoren, Wang Chonghui, Yu Youren, Tang Shaoyi
	The Imperial Party	Yi Kuang, Zhang Xun, Zhang Zuolin
	The Democratic Party	Tang Hualong, Chen Zhaochang
	The Social Party	Sha Gan, Zhou Jixiang

---

[19] Zhou Shuzhen, *A Comparative Study of Political Parties and Politcal Systems,* Beijing: People's Publishing House, 2001, page 268

March 1913 to January 1914	The Progressive Party	Liang Qichao, Li Yuanhong, Zhang Jian, Wu Tingfang
	The Civic Party of China	Zhang Naduo, Xu Jingming
	The Political Friends Party	Jing Yaoyue, Sun Yujun
	The Civilian Party	Cheng Dequan, Zhao Bingjun
	The Civic Party	Liang Shiyi, Ye Gongchuo
	Cock's Crow Society	Liu Shifu

Source: Li Jinhe, *Research on Chinese Party Politics*: **1905-1949 (Beijing: Central Compilation & Translation Press, February 2007, pages 82-96)**

The second attempt at a multiparty system failed when China defeated Japanese aggression. At that time, the parties in between the KMT and CPC, such as the Chinese Democratic League and the Jiusan Society, were strongly against the dictatorship of Chiang Kai-shek. They advocated learning from the democratic systems of Europe and America, which take the congress as the highest executive organ exercising sovereignty on behalf of the people, and take the cabinet as the highest administrative organ. In January 1946, a political consultative conference (the forerunner to the CPPCC) was held, and with the joint efforts of the CPC, the Chinese Democratic League and democrats with no party affiliations, five proposals were passed, including the *Proposal for Government Organization, Proposal for a National Assembly*, and *Draft Constitution*. This conference denounced the one-party dictatorship of the KMT. However, the KMT soon breached the political resolutions unilaterally, and overturned the parliamentary system and denied the proposed parliament, cabinet and the system of autonomous provinces at the Second Plenary Meeting of its Sixth Central Committee. The KMT had bought off several political parties including the Chinese Youth Party and the National Socialist Party to hold the discredited "National Assembly", and promulgated a constitution that supported the KMT's dictatorship. The second round of rivalries between political parties was aborted before the formal start of the ensuing civil war.[20]

2. Breakdown of cooperation between the KMT and the CPC

The history of Chinese political parties from the establishment of the CPC in 1921 to the founding of the PRC in 1949 was largely a history of cooperation and fighting between the KMT and CPC. In that period, these two parties collaborated with each other for 12 years. The first cooperation between the

---

[20] Li Jinhe, *Research on Chinese Party Politics: 1905-1949,* Beijing: Central Compilation & Translation Press, February 2007, page 335

KMT and the CPC started in June 1923 and ended in April 1927. During the first period of cooperation, all CPC members individually joined the KMT and the First United Front was built up under the three policies of "cooperating with Russia, unifying with the CPC and supporting peasants and workers" proposed by the Sun Yat-sen-led KMT. The formation of the first period of cooperation between the KMT and the CPC pushed the anti-imperial, anti-feudal revolution against warlords and imperialists to an unprecedented climax. However after the neo-right wing of the KMT led by Chiang Kai-shek and Wang Jingwei took the helm, they launched the April 12th Incident and July 15th Incident to purge CPC members. As a result, the first period of cooperation between the two parties fell apart, leading to the disastrous collapse of the anti-imperial, anti-feudal revolution.

The second period of cooperation began in September 1937 and ended in June 1946. The cooperation gave birth to the United Front against Japanese Aggression, which unified all parties and political forces to fight against Japanese aggression and to protect the Chinese nation and people. The cooperation contributed to China's great victory in the War of Resistance against Japanese Aggression. This second period of cooperation was carried out when both KMT and CPC had their own armies and governments. The coalition was based on morality rather than laws or regulations and there were "no written guidelines but only negotiations in time of trouble". After the war with Japan ended, the KMT and CPC started vying for the leadership of the united front and the breakdown of their second period of cooperation was marked by the breakout of full-scale civil war. Various complex factors contributed to the failure to develop the cooperation into a two-party system. While the main reason was that the KMT insisted on exclusive domination of political power, the two parties with their own armed forces to hand made it a top priority to seize power by force, thus turning their political conflict into a military confrontation.

3. The collapse of one-party dictatorship

After the establishment of the Nanjing-based Nationalist Government in April 1927, Chiang Kai-shek suppressed other parties by means of armed force and adopted a distorted interpretation of Sun Yat-sen's "rule by party" theory as "rule by one party", embarking on the path of military dictatorship. In March 1929, the resolution passed at the 3rd National Congress of the KMT announced the end of military rule and the start of political tutelage, and prescribed that "the KMT alone will take full charge, govern the people and prop up the political and administrative powers of the Republic of China", establishing the political system of KMT dictatorship. In 1930, the KMT promulgated the *Provisional Constitution of the Political Tutelage Period*, stipulating that "The National Congress of the KMT would hold supreme power in the political tutelage period". The KMT also organized many large espionage agencies including the Bureau of Investigation and Statistics of the Central Executive Committee and the Bureau of Investigation and Statistics of the Military Council to persecute members of other parties and eliminate dissent so as to consolidate its reign of terror. During the period of the second united front, the KMT did take some measures showing its tolerance, although limited, toward other political forces, notably the establishment of the Council for National Defense in September 1937 which included representatives from the CPC, the Chinese Youth Party, the National Socialist Party, National Salvation Association and other parties. The council had the right to deliberate major government policies before they went into effect, to make proposals to the Nationalist government, to attend policy addresses and to make inquiries to the government during the war against Japan. Actually, the council had little influence on the policies and principles of the Nanjing government and was nothing but an advisory body that had no power to alter the KMT dictatorship.[21]

Under the one-party dictatorship system, the KMT only spoke for the interests of the landlords and bureaucrat capitalists. It failed to win popular support and meet interest groups' demands for political participation, desire for freedom and need for improved living standards. Consequently, the KMT's rule became illegitimate. Moreover, the KMT resisted democracy, insisting there would be only "one ideology, one party and one leader" in China. It opposed the CPC and all democratic parties while making great efforts to boost personal dictatorship and spying activities. With substantial powers at their disposal, the KMT government and its military forces functioned with little check and supervision, becoming hotbeds of corruption. In order to monopolize all state powers, the KMT also launched a war aiming to destroy the increasingly powerful CPC regardless of people's appeal for peace. But its lax and impotent army and lack of public support resulted in its defeat in the civil war and the collapse of its rule in mainland China. After the civil war, the CPC naturally became the largest party and founded the new China

---

[21] Li Jinhe, *Research on Chinese Party Politics: 1905-1949,* Beijing: Central Compilation & Translation Press, February 2007, page 320

with its legitimate status gained by completing the Chinese new democratic revolution.

4. The establishment and development of the multiparty cooperation system under the leadership of the CPC

The CPC led the Chinese people to win the new democratic revolution and established its status as the core leadership among all political powers. This was the choice of history and the people. Non-CPC parties and democrats with no party affiliations have willingly and solemnly chosen the CPC as their leadership after long-term comparison. In April 1948, the CPC proposed to hold a new political consultative conference and establish a democratic coalition government, which received great support from democrats with no other party affiliations as well as from democratic parties including the revolutionary committee of the Chinese KMT and Chinese Democratic League. They openly expressed their willingness to join this brand-new multiparty cooperation system under the leadership of the CPC, and to make contributions to the founding of the new China. The Chinese People's Political Consultative Conference (CPPCC) held in September 1949 marked the formal establishment of the multiparty cooperation and political consultation system under the leadership of the CPC. The CPC, other democratic parties and democrats with no party affiliations jointly participated in the work of building the new China from then on. This system was created by integrating Marxism-Leninism with the practice of the Chinese revolution and by summing up the experiences of implementing various political systems in modern history. It is also an achievement of the CPC in cooperating with other political parties and establishing a coalition government. This political party system also drew nutrition from scientific elements of Sun Yat-sen's concept of "rule by party", thus the CPC's leadership position during the revolution has been passed on to its governance of the new country. And the CPC's potent organizational powers united all social groups and drew their support for the government of the PRC.[22] This system also respects other democratic parties and their positions in history, and provides an open platform to mobilize other parties to make contributions to the construction of the new China, reflecting the broad representation and inclusiveness of the new regime.

---

[22] Lin Shangli, *The Communist Party of China and National Construction,* Tianjin: Tianjin People's Publishing House, January 2009, page 59

Since 1949, the multiparty cooperation system under the leadership of the CPC has been further developed and improved. *The Constitution of the People's Republic of China* formulated in 1954 vested the CPPCC with the power of democratic oversight as well as participation in and deliberation over state affairs, formally establishing the political system of multiparty cooperation. Although this system was damaged during the Cultural Revolution that began in 1966, it was restored in 1978 and later developed and improved. Its political powers have been continuously strengthened and the system itself has become the basic political system in China. In the past 30 years or more, the status of the multiparty cooperation system under the leadership of the CPC has been constantly improved and developed by a series of laws and regulations. *The Constitution of the People's Republic of China* stipulates that this system will "continue to exist and develop for a long time", and the CPC has also passed various decisions to regulate the practice of the system, including *Opinions on Adhering to and Improving the System of Multiparty Cooperation and Political Consultation under the leadership of the CPC, Opinions on Strengthening the System of Multiparty Cooperation and Political Consultation under the leadership of the CPC,* and *Opinions on Strengthening the work of Political Consultation.*

A solemn nation-founding ceremony was held at Tiananmen Square on October 1, 1949, where Mao Zedong, elected by the First Plenary Session of the CPCC as the Chairman of the Central People's Government, announced the founding of the PRC (Xinhua News Agency)

Chapter 2

Table II. Major Events in the Development of China's Political System (1978-2012)

Year	Event	Influence
1979	Deng Xiaoping comments that the multiparty cooperation system under the leadership of the CPC is "one of the characteristics and advantages of our political system"	Multiparty cooperation and political consultation enters the phase of institutionalized construction
1982	At its 12th National Congress, the CPC updated the eight-character policy of "long-term coexistence and mutual supervision" into the 16-character policy of "long-term coexistence, mutual supervision, sincere mutual treatment and sharing prosperity and adversity"	The multiparty cooperation and political consultation system becomes an important force in securing political stability
1987	At its 13th National Congress, the CPC formally puts forward the concept of the "multiparty cooperation and political consultation system under the leadership of the CPC"	The multiparty cooperation and political consultation system is explicitly established as China's basic political system
1989	To make the basic political system more legitimate and regulated, the CPC Central Committee promulgates the *Opinions on Adhering to and Improving the System of Multiparty Cooperation and Political Consultation Under the Leadership of the CPC*	The multiparty cooperation and political consultation system is further regulated and institutionalized
1992	At the 14th National Congress of the CPC, improvement of multiparty cooperation is set as an important goal of political restructuring and building socialist democratic politics with Chinese characteristics	Multiparty cooperation becomes an important goal of political restructuring and building democratic politics
1993	"The multiparty cooperation and political consultation system under the leadership of the CPC will exist and develop for a long time" is included in the preamble of *The PRC Constitution*	The multiparty cooperation system is explicitly incorporated into the constitution
1997	At the 15th National Congress of the CPC, developing the multiparty cooperation system is included in the basic program of the CPC at the primary stage of socialism	The multiparty cooperation system becomes one of the CPC's basic programs

2000	The CPC promulgates *The Central Committee Decision on Strengthening United Front Work*	The contents, methods and supervisory power of building the political system is further standardized
2002	At its 16th National Congress, the CPC reviews its experience of multiparty cooperation and elevates this political and party system to the level of political civilization	The multiparty cooperation system as a political asset and valuable experience of the ruling party has great influence on socialist political development
2005	The CPC promulgates *Opinions on Strengthening the System of Multiparty Cooperation and Political Consultation under the leadership of the CPC*	The multiparty cooperation and political consultation system takes on a more prominent role in the new historical period
2006	The CPC promulgates *Opinions on Strengthening Political Consultation Work*	The political consultation system is being continuously improved
2012	Hu Jintao's 18th NPC Report	Integrates political consultation into the policy-making process, conducting consultations before and when policy decisions are made, and makes democratic consultation more effective
2013	*Decision of the CPC Central Committee on Several Major Issues Concerning Comprehensively Deepening Reform*	The decision improves political consultation between the CPC and other democratic parties, and also improves the system of non-CPC parties making proposals directly to the CPC Central Committee

II. The Implications of the Multiparty Cooperation System Under the Leadership of the CPC

The multiparty system under the leadership of the CPC is officially known as "the multiparty cooperation and political consultation system under the leadership of the CPC". Within the system, the CPC and other democratic parties abide by the principles of "long-term coexistence and mutual supervision, treating each other with mutual sincerity and sharing prosperity and adversity" and make joint efforts to build socialism with Chinese characteristics based on features such as "leadership of the CPC, multiparty cooperation, CPC rule and multiparty participation in state affairs".

According to the system, political parties participating in state affairs include the following eight parties:[23] the China Revolutionary Committee of the KMT, the China Democratic League, the China Democratic National Construction Association, the China Association for the Promotion of Democracy, the Chinese Peasants' and Workers' Democratic Party, the China Zhi Gong Dang, the Jiusan Society and the Taiwan Democratic Self-government League.

Table III: The Eight Non-CPC Political Parties

Name	Time of Establishment	Member Information
China Revolutionary Committee of the Kuomintang (KMT)	November 1947	Its members mainly come from four areas: those related with the KMT, those related with the democratic revolution, those related with people from all walks of life in Taiwan and others. The party mainly recruits members from the upper-middle class as well as middle-level and senior intellectuals
China Democratic League	March 1941 (reorganized and renamed in September 1944)	It is mainly made up of middle-level and senior intellectuals in fields of culture, education, science and technology
China Democratic National Construction Association	December 1945	Most of its members are representative intellectuals in enterprises, economic entities, educational and research institutions
China Association for the Promotion of Democracy	December 1945	The association is mainly made up of medium and senior intellectuals in fields of education, culture, publishing and science
Chinese Peasants' and Workers' Democratic Party	October 1930 (reorganized and renamed in February 1947)	Its members are mainly middle-level and senior intellectuals in fields of medicine and health, science and technology, and education

---

[23] In June 1949, there were 11 new non-CPC political parties in the political consultative conference: the Revolutionary Committee of the Chinese Kuomintang, the China Democratic League, the China Democratic National Construction Association, the China Association for Promoting Democracy, the Chinese Peasants' and Workers' Democratic Party, the China Zhi Gong Party, the Jiu San Society, the Taiwan Democratic Self-government League, the Chinese Association of All Circles to Save the Country, the Association of Comrades under Three Principles of the People and the Association for Promoting Democracy of the Chinese Kuomintang. Later, the Chinese Association of All Circles to Save the Country was dissolved, while the Association of Comrades under Three Principles of the People and the Association for Promoting Democracy of the Chinese Kuomintang merged with the Revolutionary Committee of the Chinese Kuomintang. So the number of non-CPC political parties in China went down to eight, as there are today.

China Zhi Gong Dang	October 1925 (reorganized in May 1947)	The Zhi Gong Dang (literally, devoted to the public party) mainly consists of representatives of middle and upper-level returned overseas Chinese, their relatives as well as those with overseas connections
Jiusan Society	May 1946	The Jiusan (literally, September 3) party's members are drawn from middle and senior-level intellectuals in the fields of science, technology, higher education and medicine
Taiwan Democratic Self-government League	November 1947	Its members are Taiwan compatriots living in mainland China, most of whom are professors, doctors, researchers, engineers and government officials

Source: http://www.cppcc.gov.cn/zxww/zxww/dptt/index.shtml (portal website of the National Committee of the CPPCC), "Column of Political Parties and Groups"

The multiparty cooperation system under the leadership of the CPC can be interpreted in three aspects. First of all, it is based on the leadership of the CPC, the decisive element of China's political system that establishes the CPC's status as the ruling party and the only party in leadership in the PRC. The CPC is the founder of China's political system and the leader of the whole political entity. Second, the system lays emphasis on multiparty cooperation; China's political system is different from the one-party or multiparty systems commonly seen in western countries. Within this system, the CPC and other democratic parties form a close and cooperative relationship based on their common interests (such relationships also exist between democratic parties). Third, the system practices political consultation, complementing the democratic election of the NPC.

1. Leadership of the CPC

Comrade Jiang Zemin, former general secretary of the CPC, defined "leadership of the CPC" in his report to the 16th National Congress of the CPC (held in October 2002) as: Leadership of the CPC mainly refers to the CPC's leadership in politics, ideology and organization. The CPC leads the state and society by formulating principles and policies, making legislative proposals, recommending cadres for important positions, conducting ideological publicity, giving play to the roles of the CPC and its members, and adhering to governance by the rule of law.

China's political power is divided into five parts: the CPC's power to lead the country is the core of the five, and the other four include the power of the people's congress (including the legislative power), administrative power, judicial power and supervision power. The power of leading the whole country is exercised by the CPC, including the power to lead the people's congress, to form the government and to lead judicial and supervisory work. In fact, the CPC leads the work of government at all levels, the army, self-governance of people in urban and rural areas, all the CPC members, all civil societies (including trade unions, the Youth League and the Women's Federation), all other democratic parties and the whole united front.

The CPC's power to lead and govern the country is exercised through CPC committees at every level, including the CPC Central Committee and local committees. CPC committees play the core role of leading all other organizations at the same level. Relationships between CPC committees and government organs and civil societies are formed and regulated under the principle of the CPC commanding the overall situation and coordinating the efforts of all quarters.

2. Multiparty cooperation

Cooperative relations between the CPC and the other eight democratic parties are based on the principles of 'long-term coexistence and mutual supervision, sincere mutual treatment and sharing prosperity and adversity'. To implement and safeguard multiparty cooperation, the CPC helps the other eight democratic parties to perform their political functions and develop themselves by providing support in policy and resources. The CPC respects and safeguards the right of other political parties to express their own opinions in their own names at all political consultative conferences, the right of members of other political parties and non-party figures to supervise government work, make proposals, report wrongdoings or illegal deeds and report social problems and public opinions. Before making any major decisions, the CPC always invites members of other political parties to consultative meetings and discussions, briefs them on decisions and listens to their opinions. The CPC ensures that members of other political parties and non-party figures constitute a relatively large proportion of the CPPCC, standing committees and leading positions of the political consultative conferences; the CPC ensures that members of other political parties and non-party figures are in all special committees of the CPPCC. Some of the other political party members and non-party figures also serve as leaders of CPPCC branches and are entrusted with powers and responsibilities.

According to the *Opinions of the CPC Central Committee on Upholding and Improving Multiparty Cooperation and Political Consultation under the Leadership of the CPC*, members of other political parties should be involved in governing the country by holding a certain proportion of leading posts in governments, administrative departments and judicial organs.

Meanwhile, the CPC requires CPC committees and people's governments at all levels to effectively assist the CPPCC at every level to solve problems in communications among its members and to fund activities. CPC committees are required to advance theoretical studies on the CPPCC and to include theories of the CPPCC in the teaching plans of party schools, academies of governance, executive leadership academies and institutes of socialism at all levels.

3. Consultative democracy

According to the *Report to the 18th National Congress of the CPC* (*November 2012*), socialist consultative democracy is an important form of people's democracy in our country. We should improve its institutions and work mechanisms and promote its extensive, multilevel and institutionalized development. Extensive consultations should be carried out on major issues relating to economic and social development as well as specific problems involving the people's immediate interests through organs of state power, committees of the CPPCC, political parties, people's organizations and other channels to solicit a wide range of opinions, pool people's wisdom, increase consensus and build up synergy. We should adhere to and improve the system of multiparty cooperation and political consultation under the leadership of the CPC and make the CPPCC serve as a major channel for the conduct of consultative democracy. Focusing on the themes of unity and democracy, the CPPCC should improve systems of political consultation, democratic oversight and participation in the deliberation and administration of state affairs, and do a better job of coordinating relations, pooling strength and making proposals in the overall interests of the country. The CPC firmly adheres to making political consultation a part of the policymaking process, conducting consultations before and when policy decisions are made, and making democratic consultation more effective. Such consultations include consultations on special issues with those who work on these issues, with representatives from all sectors of society and with relevant government authorities on the handling of proposals. The eight non-CPC political parties have the right to submit suggestions and proposals to the CPC and governments on behalf of the public interest, by submitting survey reports, proposals, or recommendations after conducting surveys on concerns of the general public and problems in politics, economics, culture and social life. The CPC Central Committee submits an annual plan for political consultation according to the work priorities of that year, which takes the form of consultative conferences, discussions or meetings. The central committees of the eight non-CPC political parties can also make suggestions or proposals directly to the CPC Central Committee.

The CPPCC is an important institution of the multiparty cooperation and political consultation system. Members of the CPPCC are elected every five years, the same terms as elected National People's Congress (NPC) representatives. Participating units and makeup of the national/local CPPCC committees (including the number and specific candidacy) are decided by the Standing Committee after being approved by the national/local chairpersons of the outgoing CPPCC committees. The highest institution of the CPPCC is the CPPCC National Committee, which elects the CPPCC Standing Committee. Under the standing committee are the chairperson and special committees.

III. Unique Advantages of the Multiparty Cooperation System Under the Leadership of the CPC

In light of the 60 or more years of political experience since the founding of the PRC, especially after the reform and opening up in the 1970s, the multiparty cooperation system under the leadership of the CPC has been proven to suit China's politics well. This system has greatly facilitated the CPC in leading the most populous and once impoverished country in its socialist modernization drive. It has also provided favorable conditions for political integration and pursuing the common interests of everybody as well as facilitated the CPC and the country to overcome all sorts of difficulties. The system has proved to be a strong political guarantee for China's economic boom and social development. Specifically, this political system has three unique advantages.

First, the system has provided stable and powerful political leadership for China's modernization drive. China's modernization had weak economic and political foundations and started much later than many western countries.

But China has been developing at a staggeringly high speed, enabling it to accomplish in a few dozen years a transformation that took western countries a century. To maintain such momentum, the leadership of the CPC is a precondition and the multiparty cooperation system provides a framework for continuous and stable leadership. Within this system, changes only occur in CPC representatives instead of the CPC's leadership; therefore stable and yet flexible political leadership is guaranteed. The ruling party has gained much experience of governing the country and gathered most social elites to serve the all-round development of politics, the economy, culture and the environment. Besides, China's social institutions remain to be improved and civic societies are still at an early stage of growth. Therefore, copying the multiparty democracy of western countries could lead to social disorder and political turmoil. The multiparty cooperation system under the leadership of the CPC is in line with the fundamental realities and current features of development in contemporary China.

It should be noted that, under this political system, the ruling party's responsibilities and obligations are very specific. The CPC is willingly responsible for leading China's long-term development. And, based on the long-term interests of the country and the fundamental interests of the people, the CPC makes policies and overall plans for both economic and social development. Such policies are relatively consistent, avoiding the short-sightedness and volatility in policies that occur under multiparty systems.

Second, the system ensures scientific policymaking and efficient implementation. China's reform and opening up is designed to achieve modernization and catch up with western countries, and therefore the method and speed are of great significance. To develop in a scientific way, the country needs to guarantee scientific policymaking. The multiparty cooperation system provides a good platform for the CPC to hear public opinions and adopt suggestions from other political parties and professional figures, thus promoting scientific policymaking. Consultation with other political parties and non-party figures has become an integral part of the policymaking process before a major decision is promulgated. The CPC is actively seeking and selectively adopting opinions from other political parties, which to some extent defies the autocratic nature of the one-party system. The constitution and other laws prescribe that non-CPC political parties have the right to surpervise the CPC, which imposes necessary restrictions on the ruling party and promotes democratic policymaking. Moreover, the system ensures consistent and efficient policymaking as well as specific division of responsibilities and well coordinated cooperation in the implementation of policies, as compared with the protracted bargaining and recriminations found in multiparty systems.

Third, the system guarantees social integration and caters for the interests of all social groups. The degree of social integration depends largely on the political system's functions of defusing conflicts of interest and catering to the needs of different people. The multiparty cooperation system under the leadership of the CPC safeguards the people's fundamental interests and caters to the specific interests of various social groups. This system gives full play to the cooperation, inclusion and consultation needed to effectively coordinate the relationships between different social groups. Some social conflicts and problems can thus be defused within this system, helping create a social environment where all people can do their best and get paid accordingly while living in harmony with others.

The system also represents the interests of different social groups. On one hand, the CPC has been recruiting members from new social classes and elite groups while at the same time catering to the interests of people from different social classes. On the other hand, non-CPC political parties under the system all have their own connections with specific social groups. In both ways, a growing number of social groups are involved in the political system, bringing more ideas and voices into the system and promoting social cohesion. This reduces the external pressures on the political system and helps to coordinate relationships between different social groups by defusing conflicts of interest. This maximizes the number of people united under the banner of advancing China's modernization drive and the development of socialism with Chinese characteristics.

In conclusion, a suitable political system must be one that promotes social progress as well as national development or, in other words, one that suits the national conditions and meets the needs of the functioning of a country.[24] Overall, the multiparty cooperation and consultation system under the leadership of the CPC has met the development needs of socialism with Chinese characteristics over the past decades and will continue to develop in parallel with China's modernization drive. For sure, China will continue to draw lessons from other countries' political achievements to improve its own political system and contribute to the world's political development by pushing ahead reform, innovation and change.

---

[24] Lin Shangli, *Political Party, Party Systems and Modern Countries – A Reflection on China's Political Party System*, Paper of China Executive Leadership Academy, Yan'an, 2009, pages 5-14

Chapter 3

What Does the CPC Depend On For Effective Organization and Cohesion?

When the CPC was founded in July 1921, it was a party with only about 50 members. After more than 90 years' development, the CPC is now a political party with more than 88 million members. As the only ruling party in a country with a 1.3 billion population and a political party with a huge 88 million or more members, the CPC faces great challenges in self-management. In this case, how does such a huge party manage to effectively organize itself to make the most of its strengths?

I. Rigorous Organizational System

The organizational system of the CPC consists of central, local and grassroots organizations as well as agencies of the CPC committees at all levels. Its organizations are all over the nation and among other organizations and social institutions at the grassroots level. All these organizations together form a complete and rigorous organizational system.

1. Central organizations of the CPC

(1) The National Congress. The National Congress of the CPC is the highest leadership organ of the CPC and exercises supreme decision-making power. It is held every five years and convened by the Central Committee.

Statistics: BEIJING, June 30, 2014 (Xinhua News Agency) – According to the latest statistics of the Central Organization Department, by the end of 2013, the total number of CPC members was 88 million. There were 4.304 million grassroots CPC organizations, including 203,000 grassroots party committees, 265,000 general party branches, and 3.835 million party branches. As for the composition of CPC members, there were 21.09 million female members (accounting for 24.3% of the total), 5.954 million ethnic minority members (accounting for 6.9% of the total), and 36.068 million members with an associate

> *or above degree (accounting for 41.6% of the total). In terms of age distribution, there were 22.376 million members aged 35 or under, 17.673 million members aged between 36 and 45, 23.597 million members aged between 46 and 59, and 23.041 million members aged 60 or above. As for the occupations of CPC members, 7.343 million members were workers, 25.703 million members worked in agriculture, livestock and fishery, 5.019 million members were technical workers in enterprises, 5.069 million members were administrative staff in enterprises, 10.88 million members were technical workers or administrative staff in public institutions or private non-enterprise units, 7.303 million members worked in the government or CPC organizations, 2.604 million members were students, 15.891 million members were retired and 6.874 million members were from other walks of life.*

The functions and powers of the National Congress of the CPC are to: listen to and deliberate on reports of the Central Committee; listen to and deliberate on reports of the Central Commission for Discipline Inspection; discuss and decide on major issues concerning the CPC; amend the *Constitution of the CPC*; elect the Central Committee; and elect the Central Commission for Discipline Inspection.

(2) The Central Committee. The Central Committee is the highest leadership organ when the National Congress of the CPC is not in session. When the National Congress of the CPC is not in session, the Central Committee carries out decisions passed at the National Congress of the CPC, directs the entire work of the CPC and is the representative of the CPC.

The Political Bureau of the CPC, the Standing Committee of the Political Bureau and the General Secretary of the Central Committee of the CPC are elected by the Central Committee at plenary sessions. When the Central Committee is not in plenary sessions, the Political Bureau and its Standing Committee exercise the functions and powers of the Central Committee. The Standing Committee of the Political Bureau is the leading unit for the CPC's day-to-day work. The Secretariat of the Central Committee is the working unit for the Political Bureau of the Central Committee and its Standing Committee. The members of the Secretariat are nominated by the Standing Committee of the Political Bureau of the Central Committee and are subject to endorsement by the Central Committee in plenary sessions.

The General Secretary of the Central Committee is responsible for convening meetings of the Political Bureau and its Standing Committee, and presides over the work of the Secretariat.

(3) The Central Commission for Discipline Inspection. The Central Commission for Discipline Inspection is the highest organ for discipline and inspection. It is elected by, and reports to, the National Congress of the CPC. When the National Congress of the CPC is not in session, the commission works under the Central Committtee. The Central Commission for Discipline Inspection is responsible for upholding the *Constitution of the CPC* and other CPC regulations, supervising the implementation of the party's lines, principles, policies and decisions, helping the Central Committee to regulate CPC members' conduct as well as organizing and coordinating anti-corruption work.

Local and grassroots commissions for discipline inspection work under the dual leadership of the equal-level CPC committee and upper commisions for discipline inspection.

(4) The Central Military Commission. The Central Military Commission was established to ensure the CPC's absolute control of the army. It is the highest military leadership organ of the CPC and its membership is decided by the Central Committee.

Chart I: Structure of the CPC's Central Leadership

- National Congress of the CPC
  - Central Committee of the CPC
    - General Secretary of the Central Committee
    - Standing Committee of the Political Bureau
    - Political Bureau of the Central Committee
    - Secretariat of the Central Committee
  - Central Military Commission of the CPC
  - Central Commission for Discipline Inspection of the CPC

Table IV: Central Organization System of the CPC

Departments under CPC Central Committee	Institutions directly under CPC Central Committee
Central Commission for Discipline Inspection of the CPC	Party School of the CPC Central Committee
General Office of the CPC Central Committee	Party Literature Research Center of the CPC Central Committee

Organization Department of the CPC Central Committee	Party History Research Center of the CPC Central Committee
Publicity Department of the CPC Central Committee (Office of the Spiritual Civilization Development Steering Committee of the CPC Central Committee works under this committee)	Central Compilation and Translation Bureau
United Front Work Department of the CPC Central Committee	People's Daily Agency
International Department of the CPC Central Committee	Qiushi Magazine Agency
Committee of Political and Legal Affairs of the CPC Central Committee (Central Committee for Comprehensive Social Management)	Guangming Daily Agency
Central Policy Research Office of the CPC Central Committee (The Central Leading Group for Comprehensively Deepening Reform works under this office)	China Executive Leadership Academy, Pudong (CELAP)
Taiwan Work Office of the CPC Central Committee (Taiwan Affairs Office of the State Council)	China Executive Leadership Academy, Jinggangshan (CELAJ)
International Communication Office of the CPC Central Committee (Information Office of the State Council)	China Executive Leadership Academy, Yan'an (CELAY)
Office of the Central Leading Group for Financial and Economic Affairs	
Office of the Foreign Affairs Leading Group of the CPC Central Committee	
Office of the Central Institutional Organization Commission	
Work Committee for Departments Directly Under the CPC Central Committee	
Working Committee of Organs Directly Under the State Council	

2. Local Organizations of the CPC

Based on the administrative divisions, the CPC has set up its local organizations at provincial, municipal and county levels all across the country except in Hong Kong, Macau and Taiwan. By the end of 2010, there were 3,222 local CPC committees all over the country, including 31 provincial committees, 396 municipal committees and 2,795 county committees.

All local CPC organizations have a full-fledged structure, including

CPC congresses, CPC committees, standing committees, and comissions for discipline inspection. Among them, the CPC committees and their standing committees are the most important and the standing committees are the leading organs for the local CPC committees' day-to-day work.

3. Grassroots Organizations of the CPC

According to the Consitution of the CPC, CPC grassroots organizations must be established in enterprises, villages, government departments, schools, research institutes, communities, social organizations, companies of the People's Liberation Army (PLA) and other basic units that have more than three CPC members. By the end of 2010, there were 3.892 million grassroots CPC organizations, including 187,000 grassroots CPC committees, 242,000 general CPC branches and 3.463 million CPC branches.

Different grassroots CPC organizations have different powers and duties.

The grassroots CPC committees in communities, townships and towns and the CPC organizations in villages and communities lead the work within their localities and assist administrative departments, economic institutions and people's self-governing organizations to fully exercise their functions and powers.

In state-owned or collective-owned enterprises, grassroots CPC organizations are the political nucleus and work for the enterprises' operation.

Grassroots CPC organizations are widely established among non-public enterprises. They are the agencies of the CPC in enterprises and play the role of political nucleus and the leading unit.

In an institution where the administrative leaders assume full responsibilities, the grassroots CPC organization acts as the political nucleus. In an institution where the administrative leaders assume full responsibilities under the leadership of the CPC committee, the grassroots CPC organization discusses and decides on major issues. At the same time, it ensures that the administrative leaders are able to fully exercise their functions and powers.

In CPC offices at every level and in national organs, grassroots CPC organizations assist the chief administrators to fulfill their tasks and improve their work. They oversee all CPC members within these offices but do not lead their work.

4. The CPC Branch

According to the *Constitution of the CPC*, a CPC branch must be established in the leading unit of central or local state organs, people's organizations, economic or cultural institutions or other non-CPC organizations. The branch plays the core role of leadership and its main tasks are to discuss and decide on issues of great importance within the units, and to take charge of cadre management.

The biggest difference between a CPC branch and other CPC organizations (central, local and grassroots) is that the establishment of a CPC branch is approved by the upper CPC organization rather than by election. Therefore, a CPC branch must work under the leadership of the CPC organization that approves its establishment.

In all, CPC organizations scattered among other organizations and grassroots units all over the country together form a well coordinated network of unity and collaboration based on democratic centralism. This network plays a decisive role in the expression of interests, decision making and implementation; therefore it is the core of China's political system. Because of this, the CPC is more than a political party as normally known in the world. It has become a public power that functions in the role of a state government and beyond. However, it doesn't take the place of the state government but improves the functioning of the state government.

II. Scientific Organizational System

How does the party manage to efficiently direct its 88 million members and 4.3 million organizations and ensure the smooth operation of the whole organizational system? The answer is democratic centralism.

Democratic centralism is the organizational foundation of the CPC's leadership. It regulates proper relationships between leaders and the people, between superiors and subordinates, between the parts and the whole of the CPC and between the individual and the organization. It guarantees the CPC's efficient administration and strong power. In other words, the CPC is not the simple combination of all party members and organizations but a powerful body united by democratic centralism.

1. Basic principles of the CPC's democratic centralism

According to the party's constitution, the basic principles of democratic centralism are as follows.

(1) Individual CPC members are subordinate to the party organization, the minority is subordinate to the majority, the lower party organizations are subordinate to the higher party organizations, and all the constituent organizations and members of the party are subordinate to the National Congress and the Central Committee of the party.

(2) The party's leadership organs at all levels are elected except for the representative organs dispatched by them and the leading CPC members' groups in non-party organizations.

(3) The highest leadership organ of the party is the National Congress and the Central Committee elected by it. The leadership organs of local party organizations are the party congresses at their respective levels and the party committees elected by them. Party committees are responsible, and report their work to the party congresses at their respective levels.

(4) Higher-level party organizations should pay constant attention to the views of lower-level organizations and rank-and-file CPC members, and promptly solve the problems they raise. Lower-level party organizations should report their work to, and request instructions from, higher-level party organizations; at the same time, they should handle, independently and in a responsible manner, matters within their jurisdiction. Higher and lower-level party organizations should exchange information and support and supervise each other. Party organizations at all levels should enable CPC members to keep well informed about inner-party affairs and to have as many opportunities as possible to involve themselves in them.

(5) Party committees at all levels function on the principle of combining collective leadership with individual responsibility based on division of labor. All major issues should be decided upon by the party committees after discussion in accordance with the principle of collective leadership, democratic centralism, individual consultations and decision-making through formal meetings. Party committee members should earnestly perform their duties in accordance with the collective decisions taken and division of labor.

(6) The party forbids all forms of personality cult. It is necessary to ensure that the activities of party leaders are subject to the supervision of the party and the people, and at the same time to uphold the prestige of all leaders who represent the interests of the party and the people.

2. An organizational system based on democratic centralism

The CPC's organizational system is based on democratic centralism, including party congresses, inner-party elections, collective leadership and organizational activities.

(1) The Party Congress System

Party congresses, the highest decision-making and supervisory organizations, have the most power. According to the *Constitution of the CPC*, the highest leading body of the party is the National Congress and the Central Committee elected by it. The leading bodies of local party organizations are the party congresses at their respective levels and the party committees elected by them. Party committees are responsible, and report their work, to the party congresses at their respective levels. The party congress system is the fundamental system of the CPC. To uphold and improve the party congress system is of great importance for party building, realizing democratic centralism, developing inner-party democracy and promoting the party's internal political activities to be more democratic and scientific.

> ***Tenure System for Delegates to Party Congresses:*** *in 2007, the 17th National Congress of the CPC decided to adopt a tenure system for delegates to party congresses and specified relevant regulations. Under the system, delegates to party congresses at all levels can take part in or initiate activities within their power and obligations when the congresses of their level are in session. For example, when a congress is in session, 10 or more delegates all together can submit written proposals or advice to a congress; when congresses are not in session, one or more delegates can submit written proposals or advice to a party committee. To ensure the tenure system works well, more ways for delegates to obtain information and fulfill their duties should be found to help them take part in decision-making, supervising the party, evaluating the party's work and maintaining close ties with the masses.*

(2) The Inner-Party Election System

The election system is an important system stipulated by the *Constitution of the CPC* and other inner-party regulations. It provides a channel for CPC members to perform their democratic rights and obligations and take part in party administration. The system also embodies the democratic centralism of the CPC. Under the election system, full CPC members (except for those placed on probation within the party) have the right to vote and stand for election. Party congress delegates and party committee members at all levels should all be constituted by elections. Inner-party election results should reflect the real will of voters and no organizations or individuals should force voters to vote or not to vote for a particular candidate. The party is working on expanding participation of delegates to party congresses in candidate nomination and improving mechanisms for candidate nomination. It is also working on reforming the inner-party electoral system and improving the system for nominating candidates as well as improving electoral methods. The party will spread the practice, in which candidates for leading positions in primary party organizations are openly recommended both by CPC members and the public as well as by the party organization at the higher level. The party will also gradually carry out more direct elections to select leading members in primary party organizations.

> ***The Mechanism of Recommending Publicly and Electing Directly in Primary Party Organizations:*** *the Mechanism of Recommending Publicly and Electing Directly, a new democratic election model for primary organizations of the CPC, is one of the remarkable innovations of the party in the past decade. Recommending Publicly means candidates can be recommended by party organizations, co-recommended by CPC members and the people, or self-recommended. On this basis, a recommending conference will be held and CPC members and the people will cast their votes to nominate the candidates for leadership in primary party organizations, which aims to strengthen the legitimacy of the nomination of candidates. Electing Directly refers to the direct election of the party secretary and deputy party secretary of primary party committees by CPC members. Voters can vote for candidates according to their own will. This election mechanism is of great innovative and historical significance as it is in line with the development of socialist democratic politics and reflects the requirements of the Report of the 17th National Congress of the CPC, which stipulates reform of the inner-party electoral system and improvement of the system for nominating candidates and electoral methods as well as carrying out more direct elections to select leading members in primary party organizations.*

(3) The Collective Leadership System

Collective leadership is the highest leading principle of the CPC. It embodies democratic centralism in the party's leadership system and guarantees the correct leadership of party committees at all levels. Central party committees and party committees at all levels should uphold collective leadership and improve the system that combines collective leadership with division of responsibilities among individuals. On one hand, the party should establish and improve discussion principles and the voting system. Major inner-party issues should be discussed and decided collectively by party committee members rather than by individuals or the minority. On the other hand, the party adopts division of responsibilities among individuals. After decisions are made collectively, specific division of labor should be made to make sure that everyone can fulfill their due obligations.

(4) The Organizational Activities System

According to the *Constitution of the CPC*, every party member, regardless of his or her position, must be organized into a branch, cell or other specific unit of the party to participate in regular activities organized by the party, and he or she should accept supervision by the masses and party members. Leading party cadres must attend democratic meetings held by party committees or leading CPC members' groups. There should be no privileged CPC members who do not participate in regular activities organized by the party or who do not accept supervision by the masses and party members. Regular activities organized by the party include 'Three Meetings and One Class', democratic life meetings, and democratic evaluation of CPC members.

The System of 'Three Meetings and One Class'. The 'Three Meetings' are conventions of party branches, meetings of party committees, and party group meetings. The 'One Class' refers to the party class. In recent years, in order to adapt to the increasing mobility of CPC members against the background of the market economy, some party organizations have practically changed the system of Three Meetings and One Class into a 'Party Members' Activities Day', when CPC members gather regularly to have group activities instead. This is an attempt to improve party activities under the new situation.

The Democratic Life Meeting System. Democratic life meetings are held every six months for party branch committees and party groups, where participants exchange their thoughts and carry out criticism and self-criticism. Leading party cadres have to participate in democratic life meetings of party branches and groups to which they belong as well as to attend democratic life meetings held for leading cadres.

The Democratic Party Members' Appraisal System. Every party branch has to hold one democratic appraisal of party members every year. In the appraisal, as stipulated by the *Constitution of the CPC* regarding CPC membership, every party member should be evaluated in terms of their performance in accordance with their positive influence on other CPC members, their evaluation by the people and CPC members as well as inspection by the party organizations. Individual party members are rewarded or punished according to the results of their evaluation.

3. Democracy and centralism are an organic, unified whole

Democratic centralism is a combination of centralism based on democracy and democracy under centralized leadership. Democracy is the full expression of the will and opinions of CPC members and party organizations and it embodies party members' initiative and creativity. Centralism is the unity of the will, wisdom and actions of the whole party. Centralism without democracy leads to bureaucratism and autocracy. Centralism loses its essence without democracy. Democracy without centralism leads to deliberation without decisions or decisions without actions. Such democracy becomes meaningless and leads to extreme democracy and anarchy as well as failure to unify the will and actions of the whole party. Neither centralism without democracy nor democracy without centralism is what democratic centralism calls for. Therefore, the system of democratic centralism that we are talking about can only be a combination of centralism based on democracy and democracy under centralized leadership.

To uphold democratic centralism, the party needs to promote inner-party democracy and maintain its vigor and vitality. It should also enforce rigorous discipline to maintain its unity.

During its long history of revolution and party building practice, the CPC has creatively used the principle of democratic centralism to formulate correct parameters and objective systems for regulating inner-party political life and relations, and this is what gives the party its distinctive characteristics in terms of organization building.

The CPC's 90-year history proves that the system of democratic centralism characterized by a combination of centralism based on democracy and democracy under centralized leadership is the most sensible and efficient system for the organization and leadership of the party.

III. Party Building Focused on Ideology

History has proved that a political party or a nation loses its goals, direction and power of unity without a strong ideological basis. The CPC is the political party of the working class which upholds Marxism to strive for socialism and communism. Marxism, socialism and communism are the political soul of party members and the strong ideological support for party members to stay unified and brave all difficulties.

1. Focus on ideology building is an outstanding feature of the CPC

When the CPC was founded, it was faced with an economically poor and culturally backward country where farmers were the absolute majority. A majority of CPC members were farmers and petty bourgeoisie. Therefore, when the party came into being and grew stronger, it was inevitably influenced by non-proletarian ideologies. Under such conditions, building a Marxist political party that represented the people became a tough mission for the CPC. Chinese communists, represented by Mao Zedong, fulfilled the task by combining the general principles of Marxist-Leninist party-building theory with the CPC's party-building practice to carve out a party-building path with Chinese characteristics, where ideological, political and organization building were undertaken in parallel while ideological education and guidance received the most emphasis. To put ideology building on top of the party-building agenda is in accordance with the objective law that human actions are controlled by their thoughts. Mao Zedong once reinforced this point by saying that ideological education is the key link in uniting the whole party for great political struggles. Unless this is done, the party cannot accomplish any of its political tasks. Whenever the revolution, development or reform was at a historical crossroads, the CPC has always put ideology building and unifying the whole party's will as its top mission. It is because the CPC has been focusing on ideology building that it has survived all the ups and downs and become a strong Marxist political party that leads the Chinese people in the right development direction.

Nowadays, many young CPC members and officials are coming into office. They are highly educated, open-minded and regarded as promising successors for the party's undertakings. But many of them lack experience of inner-party activities and major political tests. Under new circumstances, their values and behavior will become more complicated due to increasing temptation. Therefore, it is very important for us to guide CPC members and officials to have strong faith in our party.

2. Having a good grasp of theoretical construction is at the root of strengthening ideological construction

The CPC gives high priority to developing theory. Theoretical maturity is an important indicator for a political party. Theoretical awareness makes CPC members and officials firmly believe in the CPC's convictions. Communists' faith in Marxism, socialism and communism is based on their overall understanding and grasp of the truth of Marxism and inevitability of socialism and communism. First and foremost, they need to study these theories. The CPC educates its members by means of mass learning and regular learning. It also educates its members with Marxism-Leninism, Mao Zedong Thought and the Theoretical System of Socialism with Chinese Characteristics, and the party guides them to understand the world and analyze issues with Marxist theory. Therefore, party members will stay away from wrong thoughts and theories and they will unremittingly pursue the ideal of socialism with Chinese characteristics.

To let CPC members and officials share the results of theoretical development, various state-level cadre educational institutions have been established throughout China, including the Party School of the CPC Central Committee, the Chinese Academy of Governance, the China Executive Leadership Academy Pudong (CELAP), the China Executive Leadership Academy Jinggangshan (CELAJ) and the China Executive Leadership Academy Yan'an (CELAY). These institutions aim mainly at enhancing CPC members' theoretical standards and their capability to cope with party and government affairs as well as transforming them into cadres with strategic thinking and global vision. In addition, CPC members and leading officials are assigned respectively to study in party schools or academies of governance founded at three levels (province, city and county). This is an important channel for educating our comrades to master Marxist theory.

3. Education on party spirit is at the core of strengthening ideological construction

Party spirit is an inherent attribute of a political party, and it is a comprehensive generalization of a party's nature, purpose and style. Strong party spirit comes from a deep understanding of the party's history and the attributes above. Over the past 90 or more years, generations of communists, not afraid of difficulties or obstacles, fought hard for national independence, people's liberation, national prosperity and people's well-being. Numerous martyrs and heroes stood out and represented the nature, purity and fine characteristics of CPC members. The national spirit and spirit of the times are spiritual wealth from which we draw strength to overcome difficulties and obtain victories. The report of the 18th CPC National Congress noted that we should guide

CPC members to study the party's history, and gain a full understanding of the experience and lessons. We should carry forward the party's fine traditions and conduct, and require its members and officials to develop a firm and correct world view and to have a firm and correct attitude toward power and their careers, to take a committed political stand and to become better able to distinguish right from wrong on major issues and maintain a communist political character. We should cultivate party members' party spirit by requiring them to undergo relevant education and to learn from practical experience. So the CPC has established a mechanism for young CPC members and officials to work in community-level organizations and remote areas to strengthen their party spirit and enhance their capabilities.

4. Raising moral standards: the basis for strengthening party spirit

The CPC is a theoretically and politically advanced party, which is full of strength. Over the past 90 years, CPC members have drawn strength and enjoyed support from party ethics to overcome various difficulties and risks. We encourage CPC members and officials to take actions to improve themselves and be loyal to the party and become role models in practicing socialist views on honor and disgrace. We urge them to observe the party spirit and ethical standards and set a good example for the public. Recently there has been a lack of ethics and integrity among some of our comrades, which has had a negative influence among the masses. We should encourage CPC members and officials to become paragons of socialist ethics, bear in mind self-discipline, lead in fostering a social trend of honesty and integrity, uphold fairness and justice, and thus demonstrate the moral integrity of CPC members.

IV. Upholding the Principle that the Party Should Supervise Its Own Conduct and Run Itself with Strict Discipline

It is the CPC's long-term principle and fine tradition to supervise its own conduct and run itself with strict discipline. We do so to continuously enhance our capacity for self-purity, self-improvement, self-development and self-innovation so that we can overcome the Four Major Tests and Four Kinds of Danger. There are some important issues in the party at present. A small number of CPC members and officials waver in believing in the party's ideals and convictions, they are not fully aware of the party's purpose and they have become lazy and extravagant. Some community-level party organizations are too weak and lax, and so are some CPC members. All of these issues are closely related to inadequate education, management and supervision by local governments and institutions. It will be disastrous if we do nothing about managing party members. Comrade Xi Jinping, General Secretary of the CPC Central Committee, has pointed out that we must supervise our own conduct and run the party with strict discipline. Only in this way can we run the party well. We are a ruling party with more than 88 million members and we will be governing a nation of 1.3 billion people for a long time to come. We can never be too careful about running the party. If the party is badly managed and poorly supervised, and issues that people are concerned about are not well settled, we will lose the qualification to govern China.

To supervise its own conduct and run itself with strict discipline, we should work according to the *Constitution of the CPC* and its regulations. CPC members, especially leading cadres, should be strictly educated, strictly managed and strictly supervised, and they should be encouraged to observe principles and party spirit, to carry out criticism and self-criticism in inner-party activities, and to abstain from extravagance. We must recruit qualified people into the party in accordance with the *Constitution of the CPC*, fight against corruption and ensure that all members are treated equally in terms of discipline. All of these issues should be included in party building and need to be carried out in all areas.

The principle that the party should supervise its own conduct and run itself with strict discipline means that we should make all-round efforts to strengthen the party theoretically and organizationally and improve its conduct, and we should become better able to fight corruption, uphold party integrity and improve party rules and regulations. First, we should be stricter with the development and recruiting of officials. Officials should be educated, managed and supervised on the basis of tougher discipline. Every official should understand profoundly that, to be an official, they must work harder and obey rules more strictly. Second, we should be stricter with party members. We should recruit only qualified people into the party strictly according to standards stipulated in the CPC Constitution and party members should be educated and managed strictly so that they can behave themselves properly in daily life, act as role models and pioneers, and devote themselves in hard times. Third, we should be strict with the construction and management of party organizations. Community-level party organizations should be made ready to play the key role and perform key tasks. Fourth, we should be strict with intra-party activities. We should uphold and carry out democratic centralism in all aspect and at all levels. All party members and officials, especially key party leaders, should adhere to democratic centralism in their activities. Fifth, we should be strict with the conduct of party members. We should clean up the conduct totally, or eliminate any misconduct, within the party, and settle any concern of the people regarding the conduct of party members and officials. Sixth, we should strengthen party discipline to manage the party and party members, including political discipline, organizational discipline and financial discipline. All party members and officials should willingly and resolutely uphold the centralized leadership of the party and maintain a high degree of unity with the Central Committee to uphold the unity of the whole party.

To supervise the party's own conduct and run itself with strict discipline, we should implement the system of responsibility for party building. Party committees at all levels, especially secretaries, must bear in mind that party building is their fundamental responsibility. Efforts should be made to improve work mechanisms and to push party committees to fulfill their responsibilities to manage the party in accordance with strict discipline.

Chapter 4

How Does the CPC Govern the Country?

Over the past 60 or more years since it came to power, the CPC has led the Chinese people of all ethnic groups in turning the isolated and backward old China into a moderately prosperous new China. The practice of governance has made the CPC more mature and stronger. Under the new circumstances, the CPC is determined to consistently enhance its governance and improve its governing style to score more remarkable achievements.

I. Main Governance Experience of the CPC

From 1949 to the present, the CPC has weathered ups and downs and made major achievements that have attracted world attention. Over the past five decades, the party has made painstaking efforts to seek answers to three major questions: what is socialism and how to build socialism? What kind of party should the CPC be and how to build such a party? What kind of development should China achieve in a new environment and how should the country achieve it? The party has learned from its past 60 or more years of governance and has a better idea of governance in the following aspects.

1. We must make sure the party's guiding ideology will always progress with the times, and we should always use the development of Marxism to guide our new practice. Marxism is the guiding ideology the CPC should adhere to in building the party and the country. Therefore, we must follow the guidance of Marxism-Leninism, Mao Zedong Thought, Deng Xiaoping Theory, the Important Thought of the Three Represents and the Scientific Outlook on Development. We must think about important issues according to new practice and trends, direct our primary attention to major issues and emancipate the mind, seek truth from facts, keep up with the times, continuously develop Marxism and push forward the socialist cause.

2. We must continuously promote socialist self-improvement to add vigor and vitality to socialism. Only socialism can save China, and only with socialism with Chinese characteristics can we develop China. We must adhere to the socialist system and carry out reform and opening up to balance the relationship between production and the productive forces as well as the relationship between the superstructure and the economic base. We must promote harmonious development of the economy and society, promote traditional Chinese culture and learn from excellent foreign cultures to demonstrate the advantages of socialism.

3. We must always regard development as our top priority in governing the country, and develop our country to solve China's problems. We should free up and develop productive forces, boost the overall national strength and meet the ever-growing material and cultural needs of the people. This is the fundamental task of socialism with Chinese characteristics. So, we need to unwaveringly keep economic development as the key task, and strike a balance between reform, development and stability. We must push forward development of the country to promote socialist material progress, political progress, cultural and ethical progress, social progress and ecological progress.

4. We must steadfastly build the party for the public interest, exercise governance for the people, and always maintain the party's flesh-and-blood links with the general public. The CPC enjoys support from the people and draws strength from them to ensure success in all our endeavors. Only in this way can we better build the party and govern China. We must never forget that serving the people wholeheartedly is our fundamental purpose. We should resolutely punish corrupt party members and safeguard people's fundamental interests to make sure that the fruits of reform and development can be shared by our people.

5. We must stick to scientific, democratic and law-based governance, and constantly improve the CPC's leadership and governance style. Considering the actual situation in China, we must explore and follow the laws of governance of the CPC, the laws of socialist construction, and the laws of development of human society. The cause of socialism with Chinese characteristics should be led with scientific thought, scientific systems and a scientific approach, which calls for persistence in governance for the people and with the people. We must support and ensure the people to be masters of the country, uphold and improve the people's democratic dictatorship and develop democratic centralism, promote people's democracy with inner-party democracy, and consolidate and develop the broadest possible patriotic united front. We should govern the country in accordance with the law. While leading the people in making laws, the party should also play an exemplary role in observing the law and always safeguard the enforcement of the law to ensure China's economic, political, cultural and social life is governed by laws and regulations.

6. We must continuously carry out reform to strengthen party building, and keep on improving its creativity, unity and capability. The CPC must run itself with strict discipline, which is of the utmost importance to meet the needs of the times and the new circumstances and tasks. Great efforts must be made to strengthen all-round party building in order to enhance its governance capability and accomplish its missions.

The experience above encompasses valuable lessons we have learned over the last 60 or more years. The experience should also be taken as a major guiding principle for the party to further enhance its governance capability.

II. The Historical Position of the CPC

Since its founding, the CPC has undergone two major changes of historical position during the periods of Revolution, Socialist Construction and Reform. The victory of the New Democratic Revolution and the establishment of the PRC marked the CPC's first change of historical position, meaning the CPC transformed from being a revolutionary party leading people to seize power to being a ruling party leading people to govern the country for a long time. This was an objective historical process, but we went through a tortuous process to understand how to rule the country. The CPC had rich experience in revolution and it had a complete mechanism for revolution. But the party was not well prepared theoretically and ideologically when it came to addressing the questions of what is a ruling party and what is governance?

Meanwhile, internationally, the hostility between capitalism and communism affected the CPC's judgment of its own historical position. During its rule, the CPC was influenced by the mindset of a revolutionary party and followed old traditions and brought disasters to the cause of socialist modernization. For instance, the 'Great Leap Forward' in 1958, which tried to promote social productivity through political mobilization and mass movements, resulted in a severe setback for China's economy. During the Cultural Revolution, the party leadership tried to develop the economy through class struggle, but it caused social and economic chaos, and turned out to be a failure. Joining the World Trade Organization (WTO) and the establishment of a socialist market economic system marked the second major change of historical position for the CPC, meaning the party transformed from being a ruling party leading national construction under the circumstances of isolation and a planned economy to being in a situation of reform and developing a socialist market economy. The CPC has a clearer understanding of its historical position.

In February 1980, Deng Xiaoping, chief architect of China's reform and opening-up policy, raised the questions: What should a ruling party be like? What qualities should a member of such a party have? How to judge whether the party's leadership is competent? He realized that the focus of a ruling party's work and the party's governing style were different from those of a revolutionary one. He noted that a genuinely Marxist ruling party must devote itself to developing the productive forces and, on that basis, gradually raising the people's living standards. We must reform and improve the leadership system of the party and the state. He also pointed out that democracy has to be institutionalized and written into law, so as to make sure that institutions and laws do not change whenever the leadership changes, or whenever the leaders change their views or shift the focus of their attention.

Based on recognition of the party's second generation of central collective leadership with Deng Xiaoping as the core, the concept of the historical position of the CPC was publicized and fully explained at the 16th CPC National Congress. This demonstrated that the party had a clear understanding about its historical position. After the second transformation, we began to push forward the modernization in a different way, pushed forward the concept of ruling the country according to law and the concept of governance capability building, and focused on expanding the class basis and mass basis of the party. We should improve the party's leadership system and its governing style, enhance governance capability, put party building on a new footing by transforming it into a ruling party with scientific, democratic, law-based governance as well as building the party to realize the public interest and exercise governance for the people.

To sum up, only by correctly analyzing the historical position and changes of the historical position of the party can the party play a role in governance and change its role over time. Only in this way can the party promote the process of modernization with correct and scientific guidance, principles and policies.

III. The Governing Style of the CPC

Governing style refers to the way that a ruling party governs a state. It is a generalization of systems, mechanisms and approaches that the ruling party takes to fulfill its governance objectives. *The Decision of the Central Committee of the CPC on Enhancing the Party's Governance Capability* stressed that we must persist in scientific, democratic and law-based governance, and constantly improve the CPC's leadership skills and governing style, which represented major changes in the CPC's leadership skills and governing style under new historical circumstances. These changes have put forward new requirements for the CPC's governing style to deal with the changes in its historical position and governance challenges.

1. Scientific governance aims to lead the cause of socialism with Chinese characteristics with scientific thought, scientific systems and a scientific approach. It is based on the awareness of objective laws. Persisting in scientific governance requires an overall understanding and grasp of objective laws, including laws of governance by the CPC, laws of building socialism and laws of the development of human society.

2. Democratic governance refers to serving the people wholeheartedly and persisting in governing for the people and with the people. We must support and ensure the position of the people as masters of the country, improve the people's democratic dictatorship and democratic centralism, promote people's democracy with inner-party democracy, constantly improve the socialist democratic political system, enrich the forms of democracy, expand citizens' orderly political participation and mobilize the enthusiasm of the masses. Currently, there are three features of the CPC's democratic governance: First, we must uphold and improve democratic centralism, which is the fundamental organizational and leadership system of the party and the state. Second, we must uphold and improve the people's congress system and the system of multiparty cooperation and political consultation under the leadership of the CPC. Third, we should uphold and improve the system of community-level self-governance.

3. Law-based governance means governing the country in accordance with law and building a socialist country with the rule of law to base China's economic, political, cultural and social life on laws and procedures. We need to turn the party's propositions into the will of the state through legal procedures. Carrying out the party's guidelines, principles and policies should be institutionalized and written into law. We must make

sure that institutions and laws do not change whenever the leadership changes, or whenever the leaders change their views or shift the focus of their attention. At present, governing the country in accordance with law requires party organizations and officials at all levels to uphold the authority of the constitution and laws, run the country and the society according to law, and to urge, support and ensure government organs exercise their power in accordance with law.

To govern the country in accordance with law, which is the party's basic governing style, the CPC needs to balance relations between the leadership of the CPC and governing the country in accordance with law. The leadership of the CPC is the most essential feature of socialism with Chinese characteristics and the most fundamental guarantee for socialist rule of law in China. We need to exercise the party's leadership throughout the whole process and every aspect of the law-based governance of the country, and this is a basic lesson we have learned in developing the socialist rule of law in China. The party's leadership is consistent with socialist rule of law: socialist rule of law must uphold the party's leadership, while the party's leadership must rely upon socialist rule of law. *The Decision of the Fourth Plenary Session of the 18th Central Committee of the CPC* noted that we should combine the strategy of governing the country according to law with law-based governance, combine the party's leadership with coordination within the people's congresses, governments, committees of the CPPCC, judicial bodies and prosecution bodies at all levels, which carry out their work according to regulations, and we should combine the making of the constitution and laws under the party's leadership with the party's actions within the constitution and laws. We should pursue turning the party's propositions into the will of the state through legal procedures, and promote candidates recommended by party organizations to officials in national institutions. We also need to pursue the realization of leadership over the country and society through government organs, and use democratic centralism to uphold the authority of the Central Committee and national unity. All of these requirements represent the unity of the leadership of the party and the socialist rule of law. The party must uphold these requirements to strengthen the party's leadership over building the rule of law. These requirements provide the most fundamental guarantees for comprehensively advancing the building of the rule of law, improving the party's style of leadership and governance, and enhancing its governance capability.

To govern the country in accordance with law, the CPC must balance the relationship between party regulations and laws. This is the fundamental requirement for the party to govern the country and society in an institutionalized, formal and procedural manner and it is also an important part of the party's strategy to run the party according to law and to rule the country in accordance with law. To realize cohesion and coordination between party regulations and the laws of the country, we must uphold the ruling position of the party stipulated in the constitution and meet the requirement that the party must act within the constitution and laws when we enact party regulations and state rules. We must build a socialist legal system coordinating party regulations and state rules, improve the party's leadership over the state and society, and give full play to the party's leadership over the socialist rule of law.

Scientific, democratic and law-based approaches of governance complement each other. On one hand, scientific governance contributes to democratic governance and vice versa. We must practice democracy and be open to people's opinions through democratic consultation and discussion to realize scientific policy-making. To achieve democratic governance, we must have scientific thought, approaches and systems. On the other hand, both scientific governance and democratic governance rely largely on law-based governance and law-based governance provides a guarantee for ensuring scientific governance and democratic governance.

IV. Building the CPC's Governance Capability

The CPC believes that the party's governance capability refers to its ability to propose correct theories, guidelines, principles, policies and tactics, to lead in the formulation and enforcement of the constitution and laws, to adopt a scientific system and model of leadership, to mobilize and organize people to manage state and social affairs, economic and cultural undertakings according to law, to effectively run the party, the state and the military, and to build a modernized socialist country. The building of governance capability is a fundamental part of party building since it came into power.

In September 2004, *The Decision of the CPC Central Committee on Enhancing the Party's Governance Capability* was adopted at the Fourth Plenary Session of the 16th Central Committee of the CPC, which noted the main tasks to enhance the party's governance capability as follows:

1. Strive to improve the capability to run a socialist market economy

To enhance the party's governance capability, first, we must take pursuing economic development as our central task, firmly uphold and thoroughly apply the Scientific Outlook on Development, and further promote balanced economic and social development. The biggest challenge for us now is to learn how to manage a socialist market economy. After 1949, we carried out a planned economy that we learned from the Soviet Union. After 1978, we combined a market economy with the basic socialist system to boost the socialist market economy by ensuring the market plays a decisive role in allocating resources. It is a great challenge for the party. Therefore, we must strive to improve its capability to run a socialist market economy.

It is important to separate the function of the party from that of the government in developing a socialist market economy. We realize that driving a socialist market economy does not require the ruling party to direct regular economic activities, but it must coordinate and handle the orientation of the economy, concentrate on making strategies, policy-making and legislation to build a good environment for the socialist market economy. The party must realize its duty and position to steer the development of the socialist market economy in the right direction. For the government, it must perform its functions under the leadership of the party. First, it must exercise law-based governance. Second, the government should transform its functions, deepen reform of the administrative system and make innovations in administrative management to build a service-oriented government which is ruled by law.

An annual participatory consultation meeting on the public budget held in Zeguo Township, Wenling City, Zhejiang, 2013 (Han Chuanhao, Xinhua News Agency)

And we must separate government administration from management of enterprises, state assets, public institutions and social organizations. Third, officials in public institutions, namely party members and organizations assigned by party committees, must learn skills and approaches to lead and manage the socialist market economy.

2. Strive to improve the development of a socialist democratic political capability

Promoting socialist democracy and building socialist political culture is an important part of our endeavor to build a moderately prosperous society in all respects. Therefore, it is an essential requirement and a fundamental way to improve the party's socialist democratic political capability. To do so, we must balance the relationships between the leadership of the party, the position of the people as masters of the country, and the rule of law. First, we must persist with the leadership of the CPC in all organs of state power. This can be achieved by conscientiously listening and responding to people's concerns, proposing legislative advice according to lawful process when necessary, and proposing a larger lawmaking role for people. Party committees should also support organs of state power to perform their functions, promote all party members and cadres in those organs to carry out the party's line, principles and policies, and all the major policy decisions of party committees. Second, we must improve democracy to ensure the position of the people as masters of the country. Leadership by the CPC means guiding and supporting the people in their role as masters of the country. To achieve this, the party should work harder to accelerate socialist democracy in a systematic way by adopting due standards and procedures; promote scientific and democratic decision-making; and improve the mechanism for conducting checks and oversight over the exercise of power to ensure that the power entrusted by the people is truly exercised for their benefit. In terms of national democracy, we need to further improve the people's congress system, the system of multiparty cooperation and political consultation under the leadership of the CPC, and the system of community-level self-governance. To promote democratic and scientific policy making, efforts must be made for people and professionals to report on social conditions and popular sentiment by means of consultation and coordination. Third, we must improve the legal system and raise the law-based governance level. To ensure a high level of law-based governance, we must enable the standpoints of the party to become the volition of the law through statutory procedures, and become a behavioral norm and principle that the entire society abides by as one, in systemic and legal terms, guaranteeing the implementation of the party's line, principles and policies. Meanwhile, on one hand, the party must act within the scope prescribed by the constitution and the law, and uphold the authority of the law, on the other, it should supervise, support and ensure that state organs exercise their functions and powers in line with the law, and perform their duties to guarantee fairness and justice in the whole society.

3. Strive to improve the capability to build an advanced socialist culture

China is the most populous multi-ethnic country in the world and is the only one with 5,000 years of culture and traditions. Cultural issues are especially essential for the CPC in any perspective. We must persist in the forward orientation of advanced socialist culture, and create a powerful psychological motivation in the whole society to make big strides in building socialism with Chinese characteristics and achieving the great renewal of the Chinese nation. First, we must consolidate the guiding position of Marxism. Socialist culture must adhere to the guidance of Marxism and we should continue to adapt Marxism to China's conditions in keeping up with the times and increase its appeal to the people, work hard to equip the whole party with the system of socialist theory with Chinese characteristics and educate people in these theories to strengthen their ideological basis. Second, we must further improve publicity work and guidance for public opinion. We should adhere to the principle that the party supervises the work of the mass media, guides the media to reflect the party's positions and to reflect the aspirations of the people, unite positive publicity with public opinion, improve the news release system, and perfect the public emergency reporting mechanism. We should also attach great importance to the internet and its influence on public opinion, strengthening the internet management system and online team building for publicity, forming a strong positive public opinion online. Third, we need to work with intellectuals. On the one hand, we must respect knowledge and professionals, adhere to the guidance that literature and the arts serve the people and socialism, and the principle of 'letting a hundred flowers blossom and a hundred schools of thought contend'. We should focus on creating a desirable atmosphere to stimulate the initiative, creativity and enthusiasm of the broad masses of cultural workers including theorists, artists and news workers to the largest possible extent. On the other hand, we must guide them to maintain close contact with reality, life, and the public, and to stress positive publicity that holds unity, stability and encouragement as a key guideline, and unify publicity about the party's standpoints with reflection of the people's voices. We should also care about their living and working conditions, treat them with all sincerity and closely unite them around the party.

4. Strive to improve the capability to build a harmonious socialist society

As China's governing party, the CPC is duty-bound to shoulder the responsibility to build a harmonious socialist society, which requires the party to constantly improve its capability to achieve that goal.

First, the CPC must take into consideration the overall picture of the Chinese Dream of building a moderately prosperous society in all aspects, achieving socialist modernization, and accomplishing the renaissance of the Chinese nation. Every positive factor should be fully mobilized from the broadest scope to enhance the creativity of society, firmly do away with systems and mechanisms that hinder people's creativity, and build up a social environment in which people are encouraged to achieve their own career aims and be successful.

Second, the governing party must fully adapt to the new situation where people's interests are diversified, and appropriately deal with the interests of different groups, in order to prevent social conflicts caused by the discrepancy in interests among different groups. All policies that are made and work carried out by the CPC should be based on the fundamental interests of the overwhelming majority of the people, properly reflecting and taking into consideration the interests of different social groups. A sound mechanism for the communication and coordination of social interests should be established and refined, facilitating the expression of people's wishes, opinions, and requests through smooth channels, while guiding people properly, thus creating a social ambience that values stability and unity.

Third, for the management of society, solutions should be achieved through educating, conciliating and negotiating with people while legal, policy and administrative means should also be applied comprehensively. An emergency mechanism should be established with unity of command, complete functions, agility, efficiency and the ability to deal with risks correctly and handle emergencies appropriately. CPC cadres must establish a solidly Marxist mass view, be exemplary in practicing the mass line, energetically explore new methods for mass work in new circumstances, and incessantly improve their ability to work for the masses.

5. Strive to improve the capability to cope with the global situation and international affairs

With the increasing development of multipolarization and economic globalization, the ties between China and the rest of the world are deepening. Therefore, for all CPC members, especially for party cadres, the ability to cope with complex global situations and to deal with international affairs must be improved. A broader horizon should be developed to observe the world, and the ability to judge the international situation scientifically and think strategically should be enhanced, in order to make correct assessments of the circumstances, grasp all possible favorable factors and take preventive measures. CPC members should attach importance to acquiring knowledge about the economy, politics and culture to gain a better understanding of history and the current world situation, comprehending how to use international rules and conventions, participating actively in discussions on and formulations of relevant global affairs and rules, responding appropriately to the attention on China from the rest of the world, and strengthening the ability to deal with international society. At the same time, CPC members should pay close attention to various challenges and risks in the fields of international politics, the economy and culture, establish and improve mechanisms for prevention and coping with affairs, and enhance their ability to deal with unexpected international emergencies.

While promoting China's modernization, the CPC has been continuously deepening its understanding of ecological civilization. The 18th National Congress of the CPC explicitly added ecological civilization construction as an important component in the overall plan for the cause of socialism with Chinese characteristics, enlarging the old 'Four in One' approach composed of economic, political, cultural and social progress into 'Five in One', focusing on economic, political, cultural, social and ecological progress. The overall plan of 'Five in One' is the result of the incessantly enriched and developed practice of socialism with Chinese characteristics, and also the result of the CPC's deeper understanding of socialism with Chinese characteristics. According to the new plan, the CPC has attached unprecedented importance to the ability to achieve ecological progress in building its governing capability.

To build up its governing capability has been a fundamental task for the CPC since it came to power, and an enormous project requiring systematic work, which is related to the ideology, mechanisms, strategies, means, foundations and efficiencies of the party's governance. The governing capacity of party cadres and senior organizers and managers of the CPC's political activities, are directly related to the governing capacity of the CPC and the overall situation of the cause of the party and the people. Therefore, strengthening cadres' education and training has been seen as the premise and basis of building the CPC's governing capability, and great importance has been attached to it. Especially since the 16th National Congress of the CPC, in order to adapt to the demands of improving the party's governing capability, the CPC has put forward the strategic tasks of carrying out larger-scale training of its cadres to greatly enhance their quality.

Chapter 5

How Does the CPC Develop Intra-party Democracy?

Over the past 90 years, the CPC has been incessantly exploring and promoting intra-party democracy. The history of the CPC proves again and again that intra-party democracy is the lifeline of the party, which is an indispensable guarantee to ensure the creativity and unity of the party. Faced with new circumstances and new challenges, the CPC combines centralism on the basis of democracy and democracy under centralized guidance. Rooted in ensuring the democratic rights of members and based on strengthening democracy at the grassroots level, the CPC has been exploring various forms to implement intra-party democracy, widely gathering the aspirations and ideas of the whole party, and mobilizing the enthusiasm, initiative and creativity of CPC members and organizations at all levels.

Intra-party democracy refers to the fact that, in the political life of the party, all members participate in, decide and manage party affairs equally. It is primary and fundamental to ensure the democratic rights of CPC members in the political life of the party. The major principles of intra-party democracy are as follows: (1) The principle of equality. All CPC members are equal in the political life of the party. Equality is the basis of democracy. There is no democracy without equality. (2) The principle of elections. The essence of election is the authorization of power. Through elections, CPC members give power to those that they trust. CPC members and delegates' rights to vote must be fully guaranteed. (3) The principle of supervision. The implementation of power by leading party organs at all levels must be supervised by CPC members and delegates. (4) The principle of disclosure. Matters of great importance, especially significant decision-making activities, must be transparent to CPC members. CPC members should be informed of vital circumstances and be able to discuss major issues. Being well informed is the premise for participation and supervision. (5) The principle of majority rule. Decision-making on important issues must be based on full discussion, while party organizations must keep to the principle of subordination of the minority to the majority. The majority rule does not mean that the majority dominates the minority; the rights of the minority should also be respected and protected. The core value of intra-party democracy lies in the decisive role of all CPC members in the political life of the party. Intra-party democracy is realized through institution, and the effect of intra-party democracy is aimed at inspiring the enthusiasm, initiative and creativity of CPC members.

I. Ensuring the Democratic Rights of CPC Members

CPC members are the core of the party, playing a decisive role in party affairs. This role is ensured through the preservation of CPC members' democratic rights. Therefore, ensuring the democratic rights of CPC members is regarded as the basic principle for building intra-party democracy by the CPC, and is implemented in every part of intra-party democracy building.

First, the transparency of party affairs should be increased to ensure CPC members' rights to stay informed. Lenin once pointed out that it was ridiculous to talk about democracy without transparency. What is the transparency of party affairs? It refers to the disclosure of contents, processes and results of party affairs. All issues should be open to CPC members except for those involving party or state secrets not suitable for publication or that are forbidden from being made public according to regulations. Those issues related to the interests of the overwhelming majority of people should also be open to society. At present, under the arrangement of the CPC Central Committee, sound intra-party information systems, party committee news spokesperson systems, and systems for hearing and consulting party affairs and reviewing community-level party cadres on a regular basis have been created by local party committees at all levels. Community-level party organizations have fully disclosed party affairs, combined with the transparency of issues in the government, factory business, villages and neighborhood committees. A more open and transparent image of the CPC is now clear for everyone to see.

Second, channels should be opened up for CPC members to participate and ensure their rights to participate. The primary and most direct reflection of the decisive role of CPC members lies in their rights to participate. Community-level party organizations hold councils of CPC members, councils of CPC members and the masses, intra-party hearings and democratic discussions, and mobilize CPC members and the masses to actively participate in these activities, ensuring their decisive role in making major decisions. Among them, democratic discussions and hearings have revolutionized institutions. The explorations and experiences of Wenling, Zhejiang province and many other places have proven that discussions and hearings, as due processes and links for party committees in making major decisions, can help the party collect the opinions of CPC members and the masses, which greatly improves party committees' decision-making ability in a scientific and democratic way.

Third, more supervisory methods should be created to ensure CPC members' rights to supervise. CPC members are the main body of intra-party supervision that enjoy the important democratic right to supervise. Ever since China's reform and opening up in 1978, especially since the 16th National Congress of the CPC, there have been major improvements in intra-party supervision.

(1) The intra-party inquiry system has been built. The inquiry system was first put forward in the *Inner-party Supervision of the CPC (for Trial Implementation)* issued by the CPC Central Committee in 2004, as a brand-new measure for intra-party supervision, and since then it has gradually come into public view and developed into a significant measure and institutional arrangement for strengthening intra-party democracy and supervision.

(2) Complaint letters and visits have been better dealt with. For example, people can dial 12380 to report anything unjust in cadre elections and any cadre or party member's breach of party or political discipline to the organization department of the CPC Central Committee, and 12309 to national organs for discipline inspection.

(3) The intra-party review mechanism has been improved. Through various activities, including meetings of CPC members, democratic evaluations and satisfaction evaluations, CPC members have the opportunity to make comments on party organizations and cadres, and results of evaluations are open to a certain extent. Thus, a complete system has been formed to restrain the power of party cadres.

Table V: The Basic Level of Disclosure of Party Affairs in Shanqi Town, Liu'an City, Anhui Province, China (Excerpts) I.

First-level Directory	Second-level Directory	Third-level Directory		Publicity Scope	Publicity Method	Publicity Schedule	Responsible Unit
		Publication Code	Publicity Contents				
Party organs' resolutions, decisions, and their implementation.	Implementing the guidelines, principles and policies of the party, and the decisions and work arrangements of higher-level party organizations	1-1-1	1. The implementation of the party's guidelines, principles and policies, major decisions of higher-level party organizations, important arrangements, instructions and spirit	Society	Documents, websites and information boards	Instantly	Party and Government Affairs Offices
		1-1-2	2. The implementation of documents related to the interests of the masses, important decisions and policies				
		1-1-3	3. Important documents related to the interests of the masses				
	Important local resolutions, decisions and their implementation, goals for terms of office, short-term arrangements, work tasks and their implementation	1-2-1	4. The party committee's goals during term of office, focused on short-term arrangements and their implementation	Society	Documents, websites, information boards, and information display screens	On a regular basis	
		1-2-2	5. Decisions on local economic and social developments				
		1-2-3	6. Completion of the party committee's annual work plan				
		1-2-4	7. Important documents formulated by the party committee				
		1-2-5	8. Work reports to the party congress			Instantly	
	Policies studied and decided by the party committee on important constructions and projects; the use of large amounts of money.	1-3-1	9. Important decisions made by the party committee	Intra-party	Meetings and documents	On a regular basis	
		1-3-2	10. Important project arrangements				
		1-3-3	11. Use of large amounts of money		The party committee	Instantly	
		1-3-4	12. Major political issues approved by the party committee, including economic or social development goals and tasks; construction goals and plans for venues for the activities of village-level organizations; construction goals and plans for small cities and towns; goals and plans for new rural	Society	Documents, information boards, websites and visits to villagers	On a regular basis	

First-level Directory	Second-level Directory	Third-level Directory			Publicity Scope	Publicity Method	Publicity Schedule	Responsible Unit
		Publication Code	Publicity Contents					
Communications with and services for the masses	How the opinions of CPC members and the masses are listened to, responded to and accepted, and how they are helped with their practical difficulties in production and life	6-2-1	4. How cadres at the town level communicate with those at the village level; how cadres communicate with CPC members and the masses		Society	Documents, information boards, websites and information display screens	On a long-term basis	Party and Government Affairs Offices
		6-2-2	5. The work scope of civil service centers, their responsibilities and institutions; the work of service centers managing capital, assets, resources and workstations for the masses					
		6-2-3	6. The help party cadres offer to CPC members who have difficulties in life; how they communicate with, help and do practical things for the masses					
		6-2-4	7. How the opinions of CPC members and the masses are listened to, responded to and accepted				Instantly	
	How complaint letters and visits are dealt with, and how social conflicts and disputes are discovered and solved; how issues related to the interests of CPC members and the masses are handled	6-3-1	8. Schedules of cadres on open days for complaint letters and visits, and how complaints are dealt with		Society	Documents, information boards, websites	On a regular basis	Departments handling complaint letters and visits at the Committee of Political and Legal Affairs and the Commission for Discipline Inspection
		6-3-2	9. How complaint letters and visits are dealt with, and how social conflicts and disputes are discovered and resolved					
		6-3-3	10. How issues related to the interests of CPC members and the masses are handled and implemented				Instantly	
		6-3-4	11. How party cadres visit people at the community level					
Institutional improvement	Rules on procedures, work systems and their implementation at community-level party organizations; procedures and requirements formulated in intra-party regulations; the implementation of the responsibility system for the party's building; and the improvements and reforms of major institutions	7-1-1	1. The party committee's rules on procedures		Society	Documents, information boards, websites	On a long-term basis	Organization Departments
		7-1-2	2. Relevant regulations on intra-party democratic decision-making, election, supervision and management					
		7-1-3	3. Procedures and work requirements prescribed in intra-party regulations					
		7-1-4	4. Improvement and reform of major institutions				Instantly	
		7-1-5	5. Improvement of the management systems of party organizations at village level				On a regular basis	

(4) The system of combining supervision from both inside and outside the party has been explored. For example, the Nanhu Neighborhood Committee in Changchun, Jilin Province has established an administrative supervision group whereby the neighborhoods supervise party and administrative affairs, which has generated satisfactory results.

(5) CPC members' rights to defend themselves have been guaranteed. In early 2003, the Commission for Discipline Inspection of Jianhu Town, Yancheng City established a system of advocacy for cases related to party discipline, drawing experience from the attorney's defense system in the judicial office. This example can be regarded as a creative move in respecting CPC members' roles and guaranteeing their rights.

Figure 2: Democratic Supervision Procedure Table

Issues passed by villagers' meetings or villagers' representative meetings, their implementation and other party or village affairs should be made public
↓
The supervisory group for party or village affairs should examine and verify the issues above
↓
Issues should be disclosed to the public through information boards, meetings, radio and leaflets. Ordinary issues should be disclosed on open days and major issues at the time of negotiation
↓
The supervisory group for party or village affairs should collect the opinions of the masses
↓
The party branch or village committee should announce improvements made according to the opinions received from the masses within 10 days
↓
The supervisory group for party or village affairs should report their supervision and inspection work to meetings of CPC members, villagers' meetings or villagers' representative meetings on a regular basis

Fourth, the election system should be improved to ensure CPC members' rights to vote (see also section II below of this chapter).

> **The rights of CPC members according to Article 4 of the CPC Constitution**
>
> (1) To attend relevant party meetings, read relevant party documents, and benefit from party education and training.
>
> (2) To participate in the discussion of questions concerning the party's policies at party meetings and in party newspapers and journals.
>
> (3) To make suggestions and proposals regarding the work of the party.
>
> (4) To make well-grounded criticism of any party organization or member at party meetings, to present information or charges against any party organization or member concerning violations of discipline or the law to the party in a responsible way, to demand disciplinary measures against such a member, or call for the dismissal or replacement of any incompetent cadre.
>
> (5) To participate in voting and elections and to stand for election.
>
> (6) To attend, with the right of self-defense, discussions held by party organizations to decide on disciplinary measures to be taken against oneself or to appraise one's work and behavior; or have other CPC members bear witness or argue on one's behalf.
>
> (7) In case of disagreement with a party resolution or policy, to express reservations and present one's views to party organizations at higher levels even up to the Central Committee, provided that one resolutely carries out resolutions or policies while they are in force.
>
> (8) To put forward any request, appeal, or complaint to higher-level party organizations even up to the Central Committee and to ask the organizations concerned for a responsible reply.
>
> No party organization, up to and including the Central Committee, has the right to deprive any party member of the above-mentioned rights.

II. Improving the Intra-party Democratic System

1. Reform and improve the party congress system

The party congress is the organ of supreme power inside the party; the party representative congress system is the basic intra-party democratic institution. To develop intra-party democracy, the party representative congress system must be further improved.

First, the ratio of community-level delegates at party congresses should be increased. Since China's reform and opening up, the proportion of community-level delegates to congresses, particularly those elected from among workers and farmers, has been decreasing while that of cadres has been increasing, which goes against the principle of broad representation. Therefore, the Fourth Plenary Session of the 17th CPC Central Committee set forth the task of changing the proportion in favor of community-level delegates. The 18th National Congress of the CPC and party congresses around the country have seen more of these delegates. Their proportion in party congresses at all levels will be further improved in the future.

Basic information about the 18th National Congress of the CPC delegates is as follows: (1) The number of community-level delegates on the front line in various fields of endeavor has increased. There were 1,578 delegates elected from among party cadres, accounting for 69.5% of all delegates, 2.1% fewer than at the 17th National Congress; 692 delegates were CPC members on the front line in various fields of endeavor, accounting for 30.5%, 2.1% more than at the previous congress. The average proportion of community-level delegates at the provincial level exceeded 34.4%, 2.6% higher than at the previous congress. (2) The proportion of delegates elected from among workers has increased substantially. There were 169 delegates elected from among workers, including 26 CPC members who were migrant workers, accounting for 7.4%, compared with 51 such delegates at the previous congress. Among all the delegates from centrally-administered SOEs in Beijing and SOEs at the provincial level, workers accounted for 10.4% of all delegates. (3) The number of female and ethnic minority delegates has increased. There were 521 female delegates, accounting for 23%, 76 more than at the previous congress. There were 249 delegates from 43 ethnic minorities (one more ethnic group than at the previous congress), accounting for 11%, seven more than the number of delegates to the previous congress. (4) Age distribution has become more appropriate, and the level of education is high. The average age of delegates was 52, with 1,471 delegates under the age of 55, accounting for 64.8%, and 399 under 45, accounting for 17.6%. There were 2,122 delegates with junior college degrees or above, accounting for 93.5%. There were more young CPC members, with 114 under the age of 35, accounting for 5%, 1.9% higher than in the previous congress.

Second, the tenure system for party congress delegates should be implemented and improved. When the tenure system was not adopted in the past, delegates only attended congresses every five years and did not work as delegates when the congresses were not in session. The 17th National Congress put forward the tenure system, which enables delegates to exercise their rights whether congresses are in session or not, so delegates can play their roles.

> **Provisional Regulation for the Tenure System of National and Local CPC Congresses**
>
> *Chapter Two: Rights and Responsibilities of Party Congress Delegates*
>
> *Article 5. Delegates should study the party's theories, guidelines, principles and policies, spread them among the people and follow them in life. They should also study, spread and implement the essence of the party congress, be exemplary in observing the party's constitution, intra-party regulations, and state laws and regulations. They must make efforts to maintain the solidarity and unity of the party, closely communicate with CPC members and the masses, and play a leading role in the process of production, work, and study. Their powers must be exercised carefully and cannot be used for any personal interest or privilege, and they should accept supervision from CPC members and the masses with an open mind.*
>
> *Article 6. Delegates have the following rights and responsibilities:*
>
> I. *To listen to and review the reports of the party's committees and commissions for discipline inspection during party congresses at the corresponding levels;*
>
> II. *To discuss and make decisions on major issues during party congresses at the corresponding levels;*
>
> III. *The right to participate in voting or elections and to stand for election during party congresses at the corresponding levels;*
>
> IV. *To be better informed about the implementation of the party's resolutions and decisions by the party's committees and commissions for discipline inspection at the corresponding levels and the organizations they are in;*
>
> V. *To give advice and suggestions to party congresses or party committees at the corresponding levels on promoting economic, political, cultural, social and party progress;*
>
> VI. *To supervise party committees and commissions for discipline inspection at the corresponding levels and their members*
>
> VII. *To participate in activities organized by party congresses and party committees at the corresponding levels;*

VIII. To complete work entrusted by party congresses and party committees at the corresponding levels.

Chapter Three: How Party Congresses Work

Article 7. Delegates fulfill their duties through participating in activities organized by party congresses and party committees at the corresponding levels

Article 8. When party congresses are in session, delegates can put forward joint proposals within the power of congresses at the corresponding levels. A proposal should include the cause, reason and scheme. Delegates who put forward a proposal can request its withdrawal.

Article 9. When Party congresses are not in sessions, the delegates can bring forth proposals within the power of corresponding-level congresses and committees and submit to committees at the corresponding levels; the proposals should be in written form, either of their own or jointly-signed. Through participating in discussions and attending meetings, the delegates can bring forward opinions and advice on the formulation of important party documents and the making of major decisions including local economic development and the party's building.

Article 10. When entrusted by party congresses and party committees at the corresponding levels, the delegates can investigate into important relevant decisions and issues within the power of local congresses and committees at the corresponding levels.

Article 11. The delegates should take appropriate measures to better communicate with community-level CPC members and the masses, learn about the problems met in the implementation of the party's resolutions and decisions, and express the opinions and suggestions of community-level CPC members and the masses.

Article 12. The delegates can be invited to attend and express their opinions at plenary sessions of corresponding-level party committees and other meetings.

Article 13. Under the arrangements of corresponding-level committees, the delegates can participate in democratic recommendations of local cadres, democratic evaluations of the work of cadres and members at the corresponding-level party committees or commissions for discipline inspection, and reviews of the work of corresponding-level party committees' standing committees.

Third, the trial implementation of a tenure system for party congress delegates should be continued. There are three basic features of the tenure system. (1) The delegates enjoy tenures of the same length as the corresponding-level congresses. (2) Party congresses implement the system of annual meetings; one meeting is held every year. (3) The delegates participate in activities held either when the congresses are in session, or not, in an organized and well planned manner. They participate in decision-making processes and supervisory activities, set examples for others, and reflect public opinion. The permanent tenure system originated at the 8th National Congress of the CPC. But due to various reasons, it was abolished after the Second Session of the Eighth National Congress. When the reform and opening up brought a trend of democracy in China, to adapt to this trend, in December 1988, the permanent tenure system was implemented on a trial basis in Jiaojiang (county-level), Shaoxing (prefecture-level) and other places in Zhejiang Province under a decision made by the CPC Central Committee. Later, the 16th, 17th and 18th National Congresses promoted broader and deeper trial implementation for it in counties, county-level cities and city districts. The party congress annual meeting system has also been implemented on a trial basis in villages and towns.

2. Improve and perfect the party committee decision-making system

In an article *On Strengthening the Party Committee System*, Mao Zedong said, "the party committee system is an important party institution for ensuring collective leadership and preventing any individual from monopolizing the conduct of affairs."[25] The advantages of the party committee system should be further developed today. The party's democratic decision-making system should be improved to ensure democratic and scientific decisions.

Local party committees are composed of plenary sessions and standing committees. To improve the party's decision-making system, decision-making processes and supervisory activities of the plenary sessions should be strengthened, rules of procedure and decision-making processes of the standing committees should be improved, local party committees' systems to decide major issues through discussions and appoint cadres through voting should be improved.

---

[25] *Selected Works of Mao Zedong*, Vol. IV, page 1,340

Operational Institutional Reform of the Plenary Sessions at the Minhang District Party Committee, Shanghai

Since 2008, Minhang District in Shanghai has been exploring operational institutional reform of the plenary sessions of the party committee and fruitful results have been gained.

(1) The plenary sessions are held more frequently. There are four sessions annually, with one session every quarter, instead of two sessions annually in the past. The party committee believes that only when there are more sessions, can the plenary sessions play a more decisive role in decision-making processes in a real sense.

(2) More issues have been covered during the sessions. The plenary sessions used to cover the review of the standing committee's report or important appointments and dismissals. Now, more issues are discussed and decided by vote, including the general principles and framework for the next year's financial budget, the emphasis of the work of the district's plenary sessions during the year, the main leaders of party offices at neighborhood, town and district levels, and prospective candidates for the next year's department-level cadres.

(3) The evaluation and inquiry system has been put into practice. During the plenary sessions, the standing committee has to report its overall work. The party's congress at the corresponding level, the government, the leading CPC members' group at the local political consultative conference, and departments of the district party committee also have to report on their work, be assessed and questioned. At the same time, an inquiry system has been established for the plenary sessions, enabling committee members of the district party committee or the commission for discipline inspection and delegates of the party congress who attend the sessions to raise questions that must be answered on the spot to the standing committee.

(4) Specific work committees have been established for finance and the economy, human resources, party building and party congress proposals. They do not work as standing organizations but carry out investigations, inquiries and demonstrations of major issues that need to be submitted to the plenary sessions for examination and decisions, ensuring the efficiency of the plenary sessions' decision-making processes by improving the organizational structure.

(5) The voting method has been improved. Voting by raising hands is being replaced by electronic voting, and single-candidate elections are being replaced by multi-candidate elections.

3. Improving the intra-party election system

The right to vote and stand for election are basic democratic rights of CPC members. The election system based on these rights is a fundamental institution for intra-party democracy. However, it still needs to be more institutionalized and standardized in practice, and in some localities it is only done for appearance's sake to various degrees. The intra-party election system should be improved in the following three aspects. **(1) The rights of CPC members and congress delegates to be more involved in the nomination of candidates should be ensured.** As for the methods of recommendation, combined recommendations by CPC members and the masses with those of the party organization should be promoted. Election models, including the 'Two Recommendations and One Election' and 'Recommending Publicly and Electing Directly' have been created. Also, the 'Four Recommendations and One Election' model has been implemented, combining recommendations by the organization, CPC members and the masses, self-recommendations and elections by the party branch. All these measures are aimed at widening participation in nominations, thus ensuring the quality of elections. **(2) The proportion of multi-candidate elections should be increased.** By making elections more competitive, the validity of elections should be ensured. The old confirmatory election mode should gradually be replaced with competitive elections. **(3) More community-level elections should be integrated into direct elections.** The *Constitution of the CPC (revised)*, passed by the 17th

An election held in Heping Village, Tonglian Yao Minority Township, Rongshui Miao Minority Autonomous County, Guangxi, on September 15, 2011 (Long Linzhi, Xinhua News Agency)

National Congress, put forward new modes of election for community-level secretaries, deputy secretaries and other leaders, offering institutional support for direct community-level elections. **(4) More attention should be paid to technical details.** Processes and the right environment should be created to ensure that voters' opinions are well expressed in elections without any outside interference.

III. Enriching Intra-party Democracy Methods

Intra-party democracy requires various implementation methods. On one hand, intra-party democratic institutions and party leadership systems should be further developed. On the other hand, effective methods aimed at strengthening democracy passed down through history should also be carried forward, including methods of the mass line, criticism and self-criticism, investigations, studies and conversations. At the same time, new methods should be explored, including listening and consulting, and collecting opinions online. These are important features of intra-party democracy with Chinese characteristics. The following two methods are among the most important ones.

The mass line method. To follow the mass line in the party's work means doing everything for the masses, relying on them in every task, carrying out the principle of 'from the masses, to the masses', and translating the party's correct views into conscious action by the masses. As the fundamental guideline for the party, the mass line builds a better connection between intra-party democracy and people's democracy as a significant operating pattern for democracy with Chinese characteristics. Compared with today's various forms of participatory democracy, the mass line emphasizes more than broad participation of the masses, and it requires cadres and decision-makers to go among the masses and maintain close ties with them. Deng Xiaoping, a key second-generation leader of the CPC, said that the essential reason why the party overcame enormous difficulties is that party cadres and members maintain close ties, and share prosperity and adversity, with the masses. Under new circumstances, to adhere to the mass line and mass work requires improving the working mechanism of communicating with and serving the masses, including systems for cadres' reception of visitors, visits to people at the community level and their communications with the community level and the masses. At the same time, a safeguard mechanism to maintain close ties with the masses should be established, and work procedures and systems should be created to handle and answer questions raised by the masses, ensuring that their problems are dealt with. In this respect, party organizations in many places have accumulated abundant practical experience. For example, Shaanxi Province carried out 'Three Asks and Three Answers' activities, asking for people's opinions on politics, policies and their needs, while resolving their worries, complaints and difficulties. Zhoushan in Zhejiang Province pioneered a 'grid management group service work style'. In Shanghai, Changning District started its cohesion project and Yangpu District adopted a 'community-level work method'. All these efforts have successfully explored the establishment of work mechanisms for communicating with and serving the masses, maintaining close ties between the party, party cadres and the masses, and building a better image of the party and government.

The democratic discussion method. Lenin once said that: "In these united organizations, there must be wide and free discussion of party questions, free comradely criticism and assessment of events in party life."[26] The CPC attaches great importance to applying democratic discussion to consolidate different thoughts and understanding, so that ideology can be unified and consensus can be reached. Effective methods have been created, including the party committee central group's collective learning, working and discussion meetings, theory-and-discussion meetings, and discussions aimed at emancipating the mind. For example, after the Cultural Revolution, discussions to emancipate the mind were carried out on the criterion of truth, on the question of 'what belongs to socialism or capitalism' and 'what belongs to the public or the private sector'. These major party issues were dealt with through democratic discussions, which were all successful cases of building consensus and unifying ideology. Since the 17th National Congress of the CPC focused on thoroughly applying the Scientific Outlook on Development, discussions aimed at emancipating the mind have been held among CPC members and cadres in some localities, laying a firm ideological foundation for deepening reform and opening up in an all-round way and promoting sound and fast socio-economic development. These discussions are part of the process of scientific decision-making, and also the process of building consensus, deepening understanding and unifying ideology.

The criticism and self-criticism method. As one of the three main fine styles of the CPC, carrying out criticism and self-criticism is a powerful weapon for improving intra-party life and maintaining the party's vigor and vitality, and also an important way of implementing intra-party democracy.

---

[26] *The Collected Works of Lenin, second Chinese edition*, Vol. XII, page 362

Criticism and self-criticism have significant meaning for developing intra-party democracy, strengthening intra-party supervision, and ensuring that the party organization and members find out and correct their problems in a timely manner. Currently, problems such as vulgarization of intra-party life have arisen in some localities and departments, which is directly due to losing the weapon of criticism and self-criticism. Criticism and self-criticism should be vigorously promoted, and positive ideological struggle should be carried out correctly, in order to achieve the goal of intra-party harmony. Holding democratic meetings for cadres is an important way to apply criticism and self-criticism to solve one's own problems and strengthen intra-party democracy and supervision.

There are sufficient reasons to believe that the Chinese Communists can creatively integrate the market economy with socialism, and successfully develop a socialist market economy with Chinese characteristics. Also, the CPC can combine excellent achievements in human political civilization with China's realities and successfully develop democratic politics with Chinese characteristics, with intra-party democracy as its main feature.

Chapter 6

How Does the CPC Manage Party Members and Allow Them to Play Their Role?

The party is composed of CPC members, who directly decide the prestige, influence, cohesion and combat effectiveness of the party. It is important to strengthen the education and management of CPC members, and make sure that all members play an exemplary and vanguard role as indispensable subjects for building the party.

Eight Duties CPC Members Must Fulfill as Prescribed in Article 4 of the Constitution of the CPC

(1) To conscientiously study Marxism-Leninism, Mao Zedong Thought, Deng Xiaoping Theory, the important thought of Three Represents and the Scientific Outlook on Development, study the party's line, principles, policies and resolutions, acquire essential knowledge concerning the party, obtain general, scientific, legal and professional knowledge and work diligently to enhance their ability to serve the people.

(2) To implement the party's basic line, principles and policies, take the lead in reform, opening up and socialist modernization, encourage the people to work hard for economic development and social progress and play an exemplary and vanguard role in production, work, study and social activities.

(3) To adhere to the principle that the interests of the party and the people stand above everything else, subordinating their personal interests to the interests of the party and the people, being the first to bear hardships and the last to enjoy comforts, working selflessly for the public interest and working to contribute more.

(4) To conscientiously observe party discipline, abide by the laws and regulations of the state in an exemplary way, rigorously guard party and state secrets, execute the party's decisions, accept any job and actively fulfill any task assigned them by the party.

(5) To uphold the party's solidarity and unity, be loyal to and honest with the party, match words with deeds, firmly oppose all factions and small-clique activities and oppose double-dealing and scheming of any kind.

(6) To earnestly engage in criticism and self-criticism, boldly expose and correct shortcomings and mistakes in work and resolutely combat corruption and other negative phenomena.

(7) To maintain close ties with the masses, disseminate the party's views among them, consult with them when problems arise, keep the party informed of their views and demands in good time and defend their legitimate interests.

(8) To promote new socialist ways and customs, take the lead in putting into practice the socialist maxims of honor and disgrace, and advocate communist ethics. To step forward and fight bravely in times of difficulty or danger, daring to make any sacrifice to defend the interests of the country and the people.

I. Enforcing High Membership Requirements to Ensure High-quality CPC Members

The power of the CPC is not mainly dependent on the quantity of CPC members, but on their quality. Therefore, the CPC attaches great importance to the quality of its members, and takes it as an important symbol of maintaining the vanguard nature and purity of the party. The party is firmly against the tendency of emphasizing quantity over quality.

Admission formalities must be strictly followed, so that the quality of CPC members can be controlled from the start. For now, when granting CPC membership to newcomers, it is necessary to earnestly carry out the principles of 'sticking to set criteria, ensuring quality, improving structure and granting CPC membership carefully'. According to the *Constitution of the CPC*, any Chinese worker, farmer, member of the armed forces, intellectual or any advanced element of other social strata who has reached the age of 18 and who accepts the party's program and constitution and is willing to join and work actively in one of the party organizations, carry out the party's resolutions and pay membership dues regularly may apply for membership of the CPC. Members of the CPC are vanguard fighters of the Chinese working class imbued with communist consciousness. They must serve the people wholeheartedly, dedicate their whole lives to the realization of communism, and be ready to make any personal sacrifice.

Members of the CPC are at all times ordinary members of the working people. Communist party members must not seek any personal gain or privileges, although the relevant laws and policies provide them with personal benefits and job-related functions and powers. This is essential for CPC members and is also a demand that the *Constitution of the CPC* makes of them.

No matter who is applying to join the CPC, the party organizations must examine one's practices and ties with the masses. It is necessary to examine whether one meets the demands laid out in the *Constitution of the CPC*; whether one is conscious of communism and is determined to fight for the cause of communism all one's life; whether one keeps in close contact with the masses and sets a good example to the masses; and whether one can willingly observe party discipline. Only probationary members who are qualified for full membership and have completed the whole application procedure will be granted full membership.

The expulsion of unqualified CPC members should be effective so that the CPC can resolutely and properly oust these members. Nowadays, a few CPC members do not live up to expectations. They are not what CPC members should be, do not lead in serving the masses, and lack a sense of discipline and organization. They are the fatal virus in the party that demoralizes party conduct and tarnishes its reputation. If these unqualified CPC members are allowed to keep their membership, the combat effectiveness and advanced nature of the CPC will be weakened, and the prestige and cause of the party spoiled. Therefore, these unqualified members must be dealt with carefully, seriously and as early as possible. Some must even be expelled.

New Mechanism of Four-Level Cooperation Established by Wenchuan County CPC Committee to Tackle Bottleneck in Enrolling New CPC Members in Rural Areas

The Wenchuan County CPC Committee in Sichuan Province has decided to implement a new mechanism to strengthen cooperation at the county, township, village and residents group level. The new mechanism will improve the recruitment of new CPC members under new circumstances by further broadening the party's view on recruitment and raising the quality of CPC members. The mechanism includes the following steps: 1. To clear obstacles at the beginning of the application procedure by changing the method of submitting applications. Applicants must conduct 'dual submission', which means they should submit their applications to both the Countryside Party Branch and the Township Party Committee; 2.

To improve the approval procedure by standardizing the examination process in new party membership admission. CPC grassroots organizations must avoid the casual practice they adopted in the past and conduct discussions on, approval and examination of applicants every month. They should admit applicants according to a strict admission system and procedure; 3. To settle the problem of lack of supervision by carrying out a responsibility system for recruiting new CPC members. The Organization Department of the CPC County Committee must stick to the seasonal analysis system, report new developments, make the requirements clear and focus on altering the admission of new members so as to avoid the political problems of 'slow development, disorderly development or no development'; 4. To settle the problem of long-term recruitment scientifically by setting macro objectives in admission of new members. The CPC Wenchuan County Committee is to improve the quality and structure of new members by setting its recruitment objectives of seeking members with middle school education or above accounting for 80% and members under the age of 35 representing 80%. It will also hold the 'three questions and three criticisms' activity, including asking CPC members 'why they are applying for CPC membership, what they will do as CPC members and what they will model their behavior on', and the practice of 'the masses criticizing party members, party members criticizing party members and party members criticizing the organization'. After the committee implements the new mechanism, the masses will be more eager to apply for CPC membership, party cadres will be more keen to serve the party and the masses, and the quality of recruitment will be greatly improved.

102 CPC Members Expelled and 120 Required to Correct Mistakes within a Prescribed Time in Shouguang, Shandong

According to the Organization Department of Shouguang Municipal CPC Committee in Weifang, Shandong Province, it finished the registration of CPC members on April 28, 2012. In Shouguang, 102 unqualified CPC members were not registered, and another 120 members were required to correct their practices in a year due to their bad performance with the number of votes they received in their democratic appraisal being lower than 60%. In early 2009, Shouguang Municipal CPC Committee started to implement a trial mechanism of maintaining the purity of the party, featuring an analysis every half year, an appraisal every year, and a registration every two years. This year, on February 1, the mechanism was implemented across the city, including 12 steps such as individual analysis, democratic appraisal, collaborative study and examination by the organization. Those who perform badly and attract less than 60% of qualified votes will have their registration delayed. Those who have serious problems and are unqualified will not be registered. The Organization Department of the Shouguang Municipal CPC Committee will examine these two kinds of CPC members one by one, and report the result to Shouguang Municipal CPC Committee and make it public. The relevant CPC committees will arrange to educate these members and pair them up with other members from the same party branch to help, educate and improve them. (May 4, 2012, Workers' Daily)

II. Strengthening the Education and Management of CPC Members to Improve their Quality

Strengthening the education and management of CPC members is a significant measure to improve the quality of the CPC, and is essential in building an educated party. The CPC pays close attention to the education and training of CPC members in the face of its strategic mission of deepening reform and opening up, and speeding up the transformation of economic development. There are many ways to educate CPC members: 1. To carry out intensive education. For instance, in three years after the 16th CPC National Congress was held, all CPC members participated in education activities with the aim of maintaining the vanguard nature of CPC members, featuring the practice of the important thought of Three Represents. After the 17th CPC National Congress, all CPC members deeply studied and practiced the Scientific Outlook on Development and accumulated valuable experience in the exploration of equipping the whole party, instructing the party's practice, and taking forward the party's work with the latest achievements of the localization of Marxism in China under the new circumstances. After the 18th CPC National Congress, the CPC carried out the education and practice of the mass line in order to embed the value of 'being for the masses, pragmatic and clean' deeply in the thoughts and behavior of all CPC members; 2. To implement well the regular education of CPC members. The party holds the 'Three Meetings and One Class' themed reporting sessions, and specific education activities to improve CPC members' knowledge of political theory, so they can study problems from a Marxist viewpoint, and interpret and tackle real problems with a scientific worldview and methodology. The party also strengthens education about its revolutionary tradition in combination with the present conditions to help CPC members carry forward the fine traditions and style of the party and maintain a strong party spirit; 3. To put strict restraints on party organization activities and strengthen party spirit. It's a basic step in the CPC's effort to strengthen the ideological education and organization management among CPC members and a significant content of administering the party severely to put strict restraints on party organization activities. There are many important systems that can be used to perfect party organization activities, including the 'Three Meetings and One Class' system, the CPC democratic activities system, the Performance Appraisal system, the Duplex Organization Activities system and the system of regular analysis of the spirit of CPC members. The strict organization activities will help improve CPC members' sense of identity and raise their spirit; and 4. To use innovative education methods so that CPC members' education becomes more attractive. A good method of education is to make use of modern information technology such as the internet to educate party members. To strengthen the education of CPC members, the Organization Department of the CPC Central Committee has established a website for CPC members and the 12371 SMS platform, while some local organizations have launched television channels for CPC members and founded mobile party schools. These initiatives have been praised by CPC members and have witnessed good results.

Table VI: '7+5' Activity Model Promoted by Baosteel Group Party Organization (Seven Required Activities)

Number	Required Activity	Form and Method
1	CPC members are informed about the situation and tasks of Baosteel and the branch, and the requirements for CPC members are clarified	At a party convention or lecture, the senior manager reports on the situation and tasks, and the party branch secretary specifies the requirements of CPC members
2	CPC members make suggestions about the operation of Baosteel and the branch, discuss how they can excel at work next year to set examples, and develop a plan to reach the next level	These are usually conducted in group discussions of CPC members
3	A themed session on party activities is held after the performance appraisal of CPC members, and implementation of the 'plan to Reach the Next Level' is reviewed	These are usually conducted in group discussions of CPC members
4	Party members exchange opinions on study or reading	This can be carried out at a party convention, party lecture or in group discussions of CPC members
5	CPC members exchange opinions on their service for the public	This can be carried out at a party convention or party lecture

6	The party and the youth league organize joint activities	Union activity can be organized by the party branch and the league branch, or by the party member groups and league member groups
7	CPC members share opinions about their families or social responsibilities	CPC members may talk about the following topics involving family harmony, children's education, physical and mental health, environmental conservation, economical use of resources and community service at party conventions, in groups or in teams

Note: The '7+5' Activity Model promoted by the Party Organization of Baosteel Group comprises seven required activities and five optional ones. The seven required activities focus on improving the quality of CPC members and offering them a leading role in production and operation. The five optional activities encourage every party branch to propose and conduct activities of their own in line with the *Constitution of the CPC*. The seven required activities and five optional ones are to be held respectively as party activities every month.

III. Giving Full Play to the Exemplary and Vanguard Role of CPC Members

The *Constitution of the CPC* provides that CPC grassroots organizations should "give full play to the exemplary and vanguard role of CPC members, excel in performance and unite with cadres and ordinary people inside and outside the party to fulfill the tasks of their own units". CPC members are required "to implement the party's basic line, principles, guidelines and policies, take the lead in reform, opening up and socialist modernization, encourage the people to work hard for economic development and social progress and play an exemplary and vanguard role in production, work, study and social activities." In the new stage of reform and opening up and socialist modernization, CPC members should set an example in the following fields:

First, they should take the initiative to study, apply and disseminate the theories, line, principles and policies of the party, and unswervingly abide by the party's basic theory and line; and to acquire knowledge in areas such as economics, law, science and technology, and culture to do a better job of playing a leading role in spreading knowledge.

Second, they should be pioneers in socialist modernization, devote themselves to their work, strive to forge ahead and break new ground so as to make achievements that can match their identities as CPC members.

Third, they should keep in close contact with ordinary people to achieve the party's purpose of properly balancing the interests of the state, the collective and the individual, spare no effort to handle concrete affairs in a down-to-earth manner for the public, work wholeheartedly for the interests of the people, and become models who serve the people heart and soul.

Fourth, they should advocate integrity and socialist moral practice, implement socialist core values, firmly resist depraved conduct and decadent ideologies, always maintain noble sentiments as CPC members and become models of upholding socialist morals or customs.

Fifth, they should abide by party discipline, observe the country's laws and regulations, keep party and state secrets, implement the party's decisions, obey the party's arrangements, and actively complete missions assigned to them by the party.

Sixth, they should offer social care, coordinate benefits, resolve disputes, appeal on behalf of ordinary people and vigorously participate in voluntary activities, aiming to become models in fulfilling their social responsibilities and serving the public.

All these issues mentioned above illustrate how CPC members should play their exemplary and vanguard role and can be summed up in the following three statements: party members perform their duties in daily life; they stand out at crucial moments; and they will do everything for the benefit of the public in a crisis. These three sentences constitute the general requirements for, and reveal the nature of, CPC members.

The CPC should provide a platform for its members to fully play their exemplary and vanguard role. CPC members differ from each other in their social lives, jobs and personal qualities, so diversified platforms should be offered to tap the potential of each member. Maintaining high performance is a long-term mechanism serving as a dynamic that drives CPC members to be pioneers in their work, and also a regular practice for party building at the grassroots level, with the aim of creating an atmosphere of learning from model behavior and competing to be the best through awarding model behavior and encouraging those left behind. Party organizations at all levels must follow the example of maintaining high-performance campaigns to create pragmatic platforms with distinctive features based on the real conditions of grassroots units and the characteristics of CPC members' jobs. In order to vigorously promote the construction of a new socialist countryside, party organizations in rural areas must give full play to CPC members' roles by clarifying their duties and establishing highly competent leading groups to take the initiative to become rich and help others to obtain wealth. Party organizations in towns and cities must combine maintaining high performance with party building at the district, sub-district and community level based on the experience of grassroots organizations in rural areas, and give full play to CPC members' role through creating role models and organizing voluntary activities. Party organizations in state-owned enterprises and financial institutions may identify the area of responsibility of party members and launch brand projects or key projects designed for CPC members to allow them to perform their duties. Party organizations in government institutions must integrate maintaining high performance with a series of activities to clarify the nature of the party, advocate decent behavior and promote exemplary practice, such as appraising progressive CPC members and exemplary departments led by CPC members, and these will improve attitudes and efficiency in work. Party organizations in public service institutions in the fields of scientific research, culture, healthcare, and sports in middle vocational schools and in primary and middle schools should launch vocational development programs according to their own actual circumstances, including establishing Party member pioneer teams to research in key projects and reward party members who excel in both moral character and professional skills, such as Artists Distinguished for Both Art and Morality, Angels in White Gratifying the People, and Model Teachers. These programs will raise workers' ideological awareness, and improve the quality of their work and service. Party organizations in non-public economic and social entities should provide platforms to promote production and upgrade operations. To achieve this goal, they may enhance competition among party members and inspire them to work harder. As for CPC members who have no official posts, the party can establish platforms on the basis of their jobs and specialities. They may strive to become progressive CPC members, identify their areas of responsibility as CPC members and make contributions to policy publicity, civil mediation and morality appraisal. Besides, the party should carry out a broad range of voluntary programs to foster its members to serve the public.

Chapter 7

How Does the CPC Combat Corruption and Build a Clean Government?

It is a common task faced by all governments and political parties in the whole world and the consistent stand of the CPC and the Chinese government to combat corruption and safeguard integrity. The CPC and the Chinese government adhere to the principle of addressing both the symptoms and the root causes of corruption, and taking comprehensive measures to rectify both, combining punishment with prevention while focusing on the latter. They have set up a system for corruption punishment and prevention and gradually built a long-term mechanism of education to prevent corruption, a system to combat corruption and build a clean government, and a mechanism to monitor the exercise of power. A new way with Chinese characteristics that conforms to China's national conditions has taken shape.

I. Strengthening Education to Form an Anti-Corruption Ideology

Education is basic work for the fight against corruption and construction of a clean government. Over the years, the CPC and the Chinese government have unremittingly carried out education among party and government cadres and state functionaries to perform their official duties with integrity and developed a culture of integrity throughout the country. This helps to enhance the sense of honesty and self-discipline among party and government cadres and state functionaries, and to foster a good social habit of upholding integrity.

China attaches importance to education and training in integrity among state functionaries, fortifying the ideological and moral line of defense against corruption. The *Regulations for Cadre Education and Training* (formulated in 2006 and amended in 2015) and a nationwide plan for cadre education and training have been formulated, stipulating that the performance of official duties with integrity should be the key content of such education and training. Honest performance of official duties as a required course for leading cadres of all levels has been incorporated into the teaching plans of the CPC's party schools, the government's schools of administration at all levels, and other organizations for cadre training. In China, 50 national bases for anti-corruption education have been established to compile related textbooks and carry out efficient on-the-job education and training in this regard. Training in clean administration has been held for newly elected or appointed leading cadres and newly recruited state functionaries before they take up office, and files have been created for such training. In some provinces (and autonomous regions or municipalities directly under the central government), examinations in laws and regulations related to clean government are held for candidates before they are selected to take leading positions, and passing such examinations is an important qualification for such positions. As a precautionary measure, interviews about clean government are necessary for would-be leading cadres before they assume office.

1. Education in the CPC's ideals, convictions and goals

The education in ideals, convictions and objectives of the CPC is the basic element of anti-corruption education. The CPC always carries out the construction of ideological theory as its fundamental task, and educates and guides its members to strengthen their ideals and convictions and to faithfully devote themselves to building communism and socialism with Chinese characteristics. Xi Jinping has emphasized that the primary task of cadre education and training is to promote education in ideals and convictions that can maintain China's socialist system, the CPC's status as the party in power, and China's course of development. He has also stressed that education in Marxist theory makes CPC members aware of where the party comes from, where its roots are and where it is going.

It is always essential for CPC members to be resolute in their ideals and convictions, and to stick to the pursuit of the communist party spirit. The political soul of CPC members lies in their belief in Marxism, socialism and communism. Such belief can support them to withstand any test. President Xi Jinping says that ideals and convictions are to CPC members what calcium is to human beings, and that if their ideals and convictions are non-existent or shaky, CPC members will lack significant spiritual support. The core reason that some CPC members and cadres make various mistakes is the loss of convictions.

2. Education in state laws and regulations, and in party and government discipline

China makes education in state laws and regulations as well as party and government discipline routine work in anti-corruption education for CPC members and state functionaries. The Politburo of the CPC Central Committee regularly organizes group studies of the law, and this has played an exemplary role in enhancing the legal awareness of the general public, and especially of CPC members and state functionaries. It has now become a rule for party organizations at all levels and state organs to hold such group studies.

The Chinese government has energetically promoted nationwide education in general knowledge of the law. Since 1986, it has consecutively carried out six five-year plans of such education among more than 800 million people, especially leading cadres, thus enhancing the awareness of the general public about the rule of law and the sense of the state organs and state functionaries in accepting supervision during their performance of official duties. Currently the government is implementing the sixth five-year plan promoting legal education, and requires all public servants, especially leading cadres, to play a leading role in the study of the *Constitution of the PRC* and other laws. This will improve their legal awareness and drive them to rule the country in a scientific and democratic manner, and in accordance with the law.

3. Education in core socialist values and moral character

Education in clean government also advocates core socialist values and socialist morals. They are an integral part of anti-corruption education.

At the 18th National Congress of the CPC, the party proposed the strengthening of core socialist values by "promoting prosperity, democracy, civility and harmony, upholding freedom, equality, justice and the rule of law, and advocating patriotism, dedication, integrity and friendship". The Central Committee of the CPC demands that all CPC members and cadres must take the lead in studying and upholding core socialist values, and inspire and motivate the masses with their exemplary behavior and noble character.

Integrity and professional competence constitute the recruitment criteria of the CPC, with the former taking precedence. In 2011, the organization department of the Central Committee of the CPC issued *Opinions on Strengthening the Evaluation of Cadres' Morality*, which highlighted that integrity is the priority during cadre selection and will foster personal development and a successful career. Morality evaluation is the primary criterion in selecting and appointing cadres, featuring social, professional, individual and family ethics to ensure that they are loyal to the CPC, willing to serve the people and exercise strict self-discipline.

4. Education through encouragement and warning

Exemplary CPC members and state functionaries and their meritorious deeds will be praised through news coverage, films, television programs and speeches. Alarm bells will be rung for CPC members, cadres and state functionaries by compiling typical cases, shooting videos warning people against corrupt behavior, establishing education bases, holding relevant exhibitions and organizing corrupt officials to give speeches on their own experiences to fend off any possible misconduct.

5. Building a culture of integrity

The *Opinions on Strengthening Construction of a Culture of Integrity* have been worked out to promote a culture of integrity in government institutions, communities, households, schools, enterprises and rural villages. Through cultural activities and influence, the ideological and moral line of defense against corruption will be fortified among CPC members, and the idea of integrity rooted deeply in people's minds.

The party strives to incorporate integrity into the construction of popular culture and national education in aspects such as social, professional, individual and family ethics, in order to raise the anti-corruption awareness of the whole society. In accordance with prevailing demands, the party utilizes art works welcomed by the public to present a culture of integrity and encourages the production of an array of excellent art works with profound themes and that are visually entertaining. The party focuses on how to promote the dissemination of a culture of integrity by exploiting audience-friendly means of communication.

6. Publicity and guidance of public opinion

The party incorporates construction of a clean government and anti-corruption education into the annual arrangement and overall plan of its publicity. It promotes the principles, policies, decisions and achievements in these respects. Columns and special topics on combating corruption and building a clean government have been made by party newspapers and journals, radio and television stations and key news websites. Efforts must be made to adhere to the correct direction of public opinion and improve the working mechanism of net-mediated public opinion on combating corruption. The party strives to upgrade the press release system, to strictly enforce discipline regarding promotion and to strengthen foreign-related publicity.

II. Imposing Severe Punishment to Prevent Corruption

1. Self-discipline and strict governance

The party can only win people's trust and favor with a clean government and the just exercise of power. To always maintain the vigor and vitality of the CPC and China, greater efforts must be made to administer the party more strictly, to continuously improve the party's leadership and governance capability, and the party's ability to resist corruption, to strengthen the prevention of degeneration and ward off risks, and to enhance the capacity for self-purity, self-improvement, self-innovation and self-development.

It is the major political mission of the CPC to resolutely punish and effectively prevent corruption. The party should impose strict discipline on its members and firmly oppose and prevent corruption to boost reforms and opening up, and the socialist market economy. If corruption is not curbed, it will do fatal harm to the party and even lead to the downfall of the CPC and China.

It is the common desire of all CPC members and the masses to firmly punish corruption. As Xi Jinping points out, while we have made achievements in combating corruption, we must be aware that the soil that generates corruption has not been eradicated, the anti-corruption situation is very serious, and we need to get rid of bad practices and corruption that can cause negative effects. All CPC members must realize that the mission to combat corruption is long-term, complicated and arduous, and they must spare no efforts to improve the party's style of work, to build a clean government and to fight against corruption with firm determination.

2. Zero tolerance for corruption

The party keeps on taking strong measures to punish corruption, has zero tolerance for corruption and firmly prevents corruption from spreading.

Anyone who is convicted of graft is liable to punishment. Xi Jinping demands that every party member should fix in mind that once they commit corruption, they will surely be cracked down on. They should endeavor to follow the example of those who do good deeds and avoid evil practices just like freeing their hands from being dipped in hot water. Leading cadres should have reverence and take no chances. Between November 2007 and June 2012, China's CPC committees for discipline inspection at all levels filed 643,759 cases, solved 639,068 cases, and took disciplinary or administrative sanctions against 668,429 offenders, including 24,584 suspected criminals handed over to judicial organs. In 2013, committees for discipline inspection at all levels received 1,950,374 reports via the petition system, among which 1,220,191 were accusations. They filed 172,532 cases, solved 173,186 cases and punished 182,038 culprits. In the same year, China's procuratorial organs at all levels filed and investigated 37,551 cases involving 51,306 officials who committed crimes by taking advantage of their duties; these represented increases of 9.4% and 8.4% respectively over the previous year.

The party keeps on taking down corrupt officials as early as possible to stop them from committing bigger crimes. For the sake of the party's cause and the cadres, it is necessary to investigate, educate and punish party cadres at the early stage of their crimes to prevent more wrongdoing. Once there is a clue to any malpractice, the party verifies with the person involved or the relevant organization with no delay through interviews or written inquiries, and warns the person not to make any more mistakes. Those who conduct supervision and management loosely, thereby leading members of leadership bodies or their direct subordinates to violate party discipline or laws, will be held responsible.

3. Cracking down on both tigers and flies

The party is committed to taking down both tigers and flies. Everybody is equal before party discipline and state laws. No matter who you are or what your position is, once you break the party discipline and state laws, you will be investigated thoroughly and be punished.

Since 1987, more than 150 officials at or above provincial level have been punished for graft. Among them are Cheng Kejie, former Vice Chairman of the Standing Committee of the National People's Congress, Chen Xitong, former member of the Political Bureau of the CPC Central Committee and Secretary of the CPC Beijing Municipal Committee, Chen Liangyu, former member of the Political Bureau of the CPC Central Committee and Secretary of the CPC Shanghai Municipal Committee, and Bo Xilai, former member of the Political Bureau of the CPC Central Committee and Secretary of the CPC Chongqing Municipal Committee. Since the 18th CPC National Congress at the end of 2012, at least a dozen officials at provincial level have been sacked in a year, highlighting the Central Government's resolve in cracking down on corruption.

> Fox Hunt 2014: Fox Hunt 2014 is China's overseas anti-corruption campaign launched by China's public security organs to arrest suspected financial criminals escaping to foreign countries. On July 22, 2014, the Ministry of Public Security held a teleconference to deploy all public security organs to intensively roll out the Fox Hunt 2014 campaign from that day until the end of the year. On December 4, 2014, the Ministry of Public Security held a teleconference before the final combat of the operation. It also reported to the public its latest victories. During the 135-day campaign, 428 suspected economic criminals who had fled to 60 countries and regions were brought back.

China has prioritized certain types of cases to be investigated and handled in response to the characteristics of corruption in different periods. In the 1980s, the crackdown was mainly aimed at serious economic crimes and speculative buying and selling by taking advantage of the two-tier pricing system. In the 1990s, the focus shifted to breaches of the law and discipline by leading cadres in party and government organizations, administrative and law-enforcement agencies, judicial organs, economic management departments, and those above county (division) level. The emphasis was placed on investigating and dealing with cases of embezzlement, misappropriation of public funds, negligence and dereliction of duty, taking bribes and bending the law, and other official misbehavior and degeneration, especially in the fields of finance, real estate and engineering construction. In the 21st century, while making continuous efforts to handle cases in the above-mentioned aspects, the focus has fallen into four categories: 1. Cases in which leading cadres take advantage of their control over personnel administration, judicial powers, right to administrative examination and approval, and right to administrative law enforcement, to act in collusion with law-breaking businessmen, to trade power for money and to solicit and take bribes; 2. Cases in which leading cadres provide protection for underworld and bad elements; 3. Cases of serious infringement of the people's interests; and 4. Cases of corruption that cause mass disturbance and major accidents due to negligence.

4. Resolving corruption that affects people's livelihood

Corruption related to people's livelihood damages the people's interests, and for this reason people are more concerned about it. The party can only win people's trust and support by striving to cope with this problem and enabling people to enjoy the benefits of anti-corruption campaigns. This is the perpetual strong driving force for building a clean government.

The CPC and the Chinese government have made the rectification of misconduct that harms the interests of the people one of the major tasks in the fight against corruption. In recent years, the central government and local authorities have taken effective measures to achieve that by resolving issues concerning the people's wellbeing, such as the social security system, the education and medical system, low-income housing, the requisition of rural land and environmental protection, strictly investigating and punishing CPC members who abuse power for personal gain, and clamping down on arbitrary price hikes, charges, fines, requisition of donations and solicitation.

A special campaign is the most powerful measure to crack down on corruption concerning people's livelihood. For the past few years, the party has prohibited overseas travel with public funds and strengthened the management of official overseas visits. As a result, the number of groups of party and government officials on official overseas visits, and the amount spent on such visits, have dropped sharply. The Central Committee of the CPC has successfully launched a campaign to combat corruption in engineering construction and to clamp down on unauthorized departmental coffers. In December 2012, the newly-elected Political Bureau of the CPC prescribed eight rules on how to improve the party's style of work and keep close ties with the masses, highlighting its great resolve to effectively solve problems arousing intense public concern and to maintain close ties with the masses. The Political Bureau asked CPC members to practice strict economy and to act in accordance with the party's rules on performing official duties with integrity and with the rules on material benefits in such aspects as housing and transportation.

5. Strictly investigating and punishing corruption in the selection and appointment of cadres

Graft in the selection and appointment of cadres is at the very root of all corruption. China insists on the principle of the party taking control of cadres.

The party sticks to the right guidance on selection in order to recruit decent cadres. The party is also determined to bring those who break party discipline on employment to justice, to rectify the wrongdoings of those craving official positions, and to severely punish anyone who is found practicing election fraud or selling or purchasing official positions. In terms of appointment against the rules, the party aims to detect the problems early, to handle them immediately and to hold both the guilty and responsible persons liable. The party upholds and improves a supervisory system in which projects are initiated to verify and penalize, in accordance with the rules and laws, those fiddling with the selection and appointment process. In order to assure fairness and justice, efforts are made to punish and get rid of cadres who have pulled strings to obtain their positions. All these measures will rectify the situation and gain the public's trust. In November 2010, the CPC Central Commission for Discipline Inspection and the Organization Department of the Central Committee of the CPC jointly issued *Taking Resolute Measures to Stop Malpractice in the Recruitment of Cadres – Notification of 12 Typical Cases of Violations of Rules and Discipline*.

Xi Jinping stresses that the core principle of party organizations is to be impartial and upright. The selection and appointment of cadres should conform to the need of the development of the party's cause. Cadres should be treated, evaluated and deployed fairly. The organization departments should stick to the principle of making sure that good cadres are well respected and employed, and that fraudulent cadres are punished and expelled. Party organizations should uphold strict discipline on recruitment and never let anyone get away with violating discipline. Whoever craves, sells or purchases official positions will be investigated and punished.

6. Strengthening the administrative accountability system

In recent years, the Chinese government has gradually strengthened the administrative accountability system with the chief executive as the responsible person. It aims to fight against unjust law enforcement, unlawful administration, defiance of orders and prohibitions, and administrative inaction and chaos, and to earnestly fix responsibility if there is serious infringement of the interests of the state, the public and citizens' lawful rights and interests in accordance with the law and discipline. In July 2009, the *Interim Provisions on the Implementation of Accountability for Party and Government Leading Cadres* was issued by the Central Committee of the CPC and the State Council of China, stating explicitly that responsibility must be fixed for seven types of acts that incur heavy losses or produce harmful effects, including serious mistakes in decision-making, dereliction of duty and ineffective management and supervision. From 2009 to 2011, some 25,000 leading cadres were held responsible for such acts.

III. Improving Relevant Systems to Prevent Corruption

System improvement is the most effective and enduring measure in combating corruption. Deng Xiaoping said: "A system is fundamental, stable and longlasting, with a great effect on the overall interests of our country. A sound system can contain bad practices, while an inefficient one can prevent people from behaving decently or even lead them astray." It is essential to establish a feasible and practical mechanism to contain the spread of corruption, to prohibit the exercise of power by dishonest people, and to leave no chance for those in authority to commit corruption.

1. Systemic and legal anti-corruption measures

It is generally recognized that corruption can be fought by multiple means including campaigns, authority and systems. Anti-corruption campaigns mainly rely on mass movements, anti-corruption authoritative power mainly relies on the leadership's will and determination whereas systematic anti-corruption mainly relies on control and regulation.

The CPC has always paid close attention to the party's disciplinary development. It ensures that there are rules to abide by through formulating a series of significant rules and regulations that cover the main fields of party activities. The party issued the *CPC Regulations on Intra-Party Supervision* in 2003 and joined the UN Convention against Corruption in 2005, indicating that China has entered the stage of institutional anti-corruption. Its major task is to reform the leadership system of the party and government, the root cause for an over-centralized power structure, as suggested by Deng Xiaoping. In institutional anti-corruption, power is restrained by rights ensuring that people can exercise the power of democratic elections, decisions, management and supervision, "institutionalizing and legalizing democracy so as to ensure that it does not vary with changes of leadership or with a shift in view or focus of the leader". In 2013, the party released the *Regulations on the Formation of the CPC's Rules* and the *Provisions on the Filing of the CPC's Rules and Standardized Documents*. From then on, the party had its first intra-party legislation law and the institutionalization of the fight against corruption entered a new era.

Laws constitute the most authoritative system and play a critical role in institutionalizing the fight against corruption. China adheres to the rule of law as a fundamental principle, attaches importance to the regulatory and protective role of laws and regulations, and continuously legalizes and normalizes the fight against corruption and the building of a clean government. At the Second Plenary Session of the Party's 18th Central Commission for Discipline Inspection, General Secretary Xi Jinping stressed that "the party must apply rule-by-law mentality and rule-by-law measures to combat corruption, strengthen national and intra-party anti-corruption legislation, and realize smooth operation of the legal system".

2. Establishing a legal and regulatory system to build a clean government

To uphold integrity, a series of laws and regulations have been enacted in line with the *Constitution of the PRC*, and a series of intra-party rules and regulations have been worked out based on the *Constitution of the CPC*, thus gradually establishing a wholesome and effective legal framework featuring rationality and rigorous procedures.

In order to ensure that leading cadres work in a clean and honest way, the CPC has issued a series of codes of conduct and ethical rules for its members who hold leading positions, and built and perfected a system to prevent conflicts of interest. The *Guidelines of the CPC for Leading Party Cadres to Perform Official Duties with Integrity*, released for trial implementation in 1997 and revised in 2010, have provided relatively comprehensive regulations governing the conduct of leading party cadres in performing their official duties with integrity in a socialist market economy, and have thus become the basic intra-party rules regulating the behavior of leading party cadres. The CPC promulgated the *Regulations of the Central Commission for Discipline Inspection of the CPC on the Strict Prohibition of Seeking Illegitimate Gains by Misuse of Office* in 2007, and released the *Regulations for Executives of State-owned Enterprises in Performing Management Duties with Integrity (Trial)* in 2009. The *Regulations on Leading Cadres' Reporting of Relevant Personal Matters* was released in May 2010, which requires more than a million leading cadres who are at and above county level to honestly report their marriage status, the nationality and employment status of their spouses and children, and the incomes, properties and investments of their family members. The *Interim Regulations on Strengthening Management of State Functionaries Whose Spouses and Children Have Emigrated* was released in July 2010.

> ### 'Eight Prohibitions' for Performance of Official Duties with Integrity
>
> *It is prohibited to seek illegitimate gains by taking advantage of positions and power.*
>
> *It is prohibited to engage in profit-making activities without permission.*
>
> *It is prohibited to violate regulations on management and use of public property.*
>
> *It is prohibited to select cadres against regulations.*
>
> *It is prohibited to seek gains for one's relatives and colleagues by taking advantage of their positions and power.*
>
> *It is prohibited to indulge in ostentation, squandering embezzled funds, extravagance and waste.*
>
> *It is prohibited to intervene in market economic activities against regulations to seek personal gain.*
>
> *It is prohibited to be divorced from reality, practice fraud, harm the interests of the people and damage the relationship between the party and the people and between cadres and the people.*

To ensure the proper exercise of public power, China has enacted a series of laws and regulations to strengthen restraint and supervision over the exercise of power by leading cadres. For example, there are *The Law of the PRC on the Supervision of Standing Committees of People's Congresses at All Levels*, *The Law of the PRC on Administrative Supervision*, *The Audit Law of the PRC*, *The Administrative Reconsideration Law of the PRC*, and *The Administrative Procedure Law of the PRC*. Moreover, the CPC Central Committee has formulated the *Regulations of the CPC on Intra-Party Supervision (Trial)*, *Regulations of the CPC on Inspection Work (Trial)*, *Interim Measures on Conducting Admonition Talks and Written Inquiries with Leading Party Cadres* and *Interim Regulations on Reporting by Leading Party Cadres on Their Work and Integrity*, institutionalizing and improving various aspects of intra-party supervision.

To crack down on corruption in line with laws and discipline, China has enacted and continuously improved substantive laws and regulations that punish criminal offences and violations of party and administrative discipline. In the case of criminal punishment, the *Criminal Law of the PRC* has defined the liabilities of corruption-related crimes, such as embezzlement, bribery, dereliction of duty and holding a huge amount of property obtained from an unidentified source. In terms of party discipline, the CPC has promulgated the *Regulations on Disciplinary Sanctions of the CPC* and supporting provisions, which clearly specify conduct of CPC members that goes against party discipline and prescribes five sanction measures: explicit warning, stern warning, removal from party post, probation within the party and expulsion from the party. As for administrative discipline, the state has issued the *Regulations on the Punishment of Civil Servants in Administrative Organs*, which provides six punitive measures–explicit warning, recording of demerit, recording of major demerit, demotion, dismissal from post and discharge from office.

China attaches great importance to promulgating procedural laws to guarantee the enforcement of the aforementioned laws and regulations. The state legislature, judicial authorities and relevant organs have enacted *The Criminal Procedure Law of the PRC, Rules of Criminal Procedure of the People's Procuratorates and Measures of Supervisory Organs for the Investigation and Handling of Administrative Disciplinary Cases*, and the CPC has formulated the *Regulations of the CPC on Inspection Work of Disciplinary Inspection Organs*. All these have provided a legal basis for the acceptance, investigation, trial and appeal of criminal and discipline-breaching cases, and established a witness and informant protection system, a case transfer and coordination system, and a system to protect the rights of defendants and those being sanctioned.

In addition, China has enacted a series of laws and regulations closely related to corruption prevention. *The Administrative License Law of the PRC, Civil Servant Law of the PRC, Government Procurement Law of the PRC, Anti-monopoly Law of the PRC* and *Bidding Law of the PRC* aim to regulate administrative discretion and give play to the market's fundamental role in the allocation of resources so as to effectively prevent corruption. *The Judges Law of the PRC, Procurators Law of the PRC* and *People's Police Law of the PRC* clearly fortify the requirement of law enforcement with justice, efficiency and integrity. In accordance with the Constitution and state laws, local authorities have also enacted and issued their own laws and regulations, government rules and department regulations, thereby improving the legal framework for combating corruption and building a clean government in China.

3. Confining power in an institutional framework

Since the beginning of the 21st century, China has adhered to the principle of preventing and combating graft through reform in view of the success of the reform and opening up. Focusing on the major fields likely to breed corruption, the reform intends to minimize institutional barriers and loopholes and strive to curb corruption at the very source.

Reform in the administrative approval system needs to be deepened. Accelerating the transformation of how the government functions, by cancelling all administrative approval procedures for economic activities under the effective regulation of the market mechanism, enables the market to play the decisive role in allocating resources and the government to perform its functions properly. Strengthening management on retained administrative approval items will improve work efficiency and eliminate rent-seeking behavior by those with political power. This may be achieved by extensively setting up administrative service centers that advocate transparent approval procedures, and by establishing electronic monitoring systems to monitor promptly, and by improving the accountability system and information feedback mechanism. China has strengthened subsequent supervision over cancelled approval items to prevent absence, dislocation and inaction of functions. At the Third Plenary Session of the 18th Central Committee of the CPC, it was proposed to define the powers of local governments and their working departments at all levels, and to publicize the procedures for the exercise of power in accordance with the law.

China has established a market system for the allocation of resources. To set up and improve the trade market of public resources with unified rules helps to prevent administrative power from improperly interfering with micro-economic activities. In fields such as engineering construction, property transactions, government procurement and mineral resources exploitation, the legal system of tendering and bidding should be improved to regulate activities in this respect to promote open and fair competition.

China has deepened reform of the cadre personnel system and promoted democracy in cadre recruitment to improve the quality of democracy. Supervision over the selection and appointment of cadres has been tightened to prevent dishonest cadres from being appointed or promoted to a higher position, and this will increase public trust in cadre employment. China has also deepened reform of the judicial system by supporting the judicial organs to independently perform their functions and responsibilities in accordance with the law, intensifying supervision and restraint over judicial activities, and regulating the exercise of discretionary power by judicial officers, so as to promote just, efficient and honest law enforcement. Reform of the administrative law-enforcement system has been deepened to promote strict, regulated, fair and proper law enforcement. Deepening the reform of the public resource trade market and advancing the reform of fiscal, financial and investment systems as well as that of state-owned enterprises is conducive to preventing corruption.

IV. Strengthening Supervision by Establishing an Anti-corruption Safeguard Mechanism

The fundamental solution to keeping power under control is to put power, government operations and personnel management in an institutional cage to ensure that the people oversee the exercise of power and that power is exercised in a transparent manner. It is necessary to build a power-exercise mechanism featuring scientific decision-making, resolute enforcement and effective oversight and to improve the system's ability to combat and prevent corruption. It is necessary to promote political integrity, and to ensure that officials are honest, the government is clean, and political integrity is upheld.

Several intra-party laws and regulations on power restraint and supervision have been issued in recent years:

- *Regulations of the CPC on Inspection Work (Trial)*
- *Regulations on Executives of State-owned Enterprises for Performance of their Management Duties with Integrity*
- *Opinions on Strengthening and Improving Inspection Work*
- *Criteria for Political Integrity of CPC cadres*
- *Measures for Reporting on the Selection and Appointment of Party and Government Leaders (Trial)*
- *Measures for Reporting on the Selection and Appointment of Party and Government Leaders from Standing Committees of Local Party Committees to Local Party Committees and on the Acceptance of Democratic Appraisal (Trial)*
- *Administrative Supervision Law of the PRC*
- *Regulations on Leading Cadres' Reporting of Relevant Personal Matters*
- *Strengthening the Administration of State Functionaries Whose Spouses and Children Have Emigrated*

1. Supervision system for power restraint

The exercise of power without supervision inevitably leads to corruption. Based on the principles of reasonable structure, scientific distribution, rigorous procedures and effective restraint, China is gradually establishing a sound power structure and enforcement mechanism featuring both restraint and coordination among decision-making power, executive power and supervisory power, so as to promote procedural exercise of power featuring transparency and to strengthen power restraint and supervision. Now, a supervisory system with Chinese characteristics has been established, composed of intra-party supervision in the CPC, supervision by the National People's Congress and the local people's congresses, supervision within governments, and democratic supervision by the CPPCC and local people's political consultative conferences, judicial supervision, supervision by the general public and by public opinion supervision. These relatively independent supervisory mechanisms form an integrated network for close collaboration.

In China, the major functional institutions for combating corruption and building a clean government are the party's organs for discipline inspection, state judicial organs, government supervisory and auditing organs, and the National Bureau of Corruption Prevention of China.

2. System of inspection tours

Inspection tours are conducted by the Central Committee of the CPC and party committees at the province, autonomous region and municipality level directly under the central government, to supervise leading organs of the subordinate party organizations and their members in accordance with certain rules. Inspection bodies have been established by these party committees to inspect and supervise leading groups of subordinate party organizations and their members with respect to the implementation of the party's line, principles, policies, resolutions and decisions, as well as the implementation of the responsibility system in improving the party's work style and in building a clean government and exerting their own efforts in being honest and diligent in performing their official duties. Practice has proven that inspection tours have served as a vital source of clues for discipline inspection departments in investigating and dealing with cases of corruption. For example, the inspection group of the CPC Central Committee has provided clues for cases involving Chen Liangyu, Hou Wujie, Du Shicheng, Huang Yao and Song Yong.

Since the 18th CPC National Congress, the CPC Central Committee has required that inspections should focus on upholding integrity and combating corruption. The major task of inspection should be finding out problems and acting as a deterrent. Supervision over leading groups and their members should be strengthened. More efforts should be made to detect corruption and violations against the Eight Provisions proposed by the Political Bureau of the CPC Central Committee with regard to political discipline, or personnel management discipline of party organizations. Inspection methods should be improved to enhance the quality of inspection – inspection group leaders should not be fixed, neither should the targets of inspections; inspection groups should be in charge of different inspection targets; a pool for group leaders should be established; all group leaders should be approved before inspection; experienced members should be appointed to join the inspection. Inspection work should also be supervised. Failure to discover serious problems that should have been identified or failure to honestly report problems that have already been found is regarded as dereliction of duty.

3. Online supervision

As of December 2013, China's internet penetration rate stood at 45.8%, with an online population of 618 million. With the rapid development and popularity of the internet, a growing number of people tend to raise their opinions and discuss problems online. Online supervision has increased and become a new form of supervision of public opinion that responds quickly, exerts great influence and in which a lot of people participate.

China highly values the positive role played by the internet in enhancing supervision. It aims to strengthen the collection, research, judgment and management of information, to check clues provided by the public via the internet so as to look into those who have been bribed on a timely basis. Meanwhile, efforts are being made to ensure that online supervision is in order and anti-graft activities via the internet are guided by the law. To this end, reporting websites have been established by some central departments and local governments. In April 2013, online reporting and supervision sections were set up and highlighted on China's major government-run news websites – Xinhuanet, Chinese Radio net, China net, and other leading commercial news websites – Sina, Sohu, Tencent, and Netease. Those reporting sections offer links to various reporting websites, including the website of the CPC Central Commission for Discipline Inspection and the Ministry of Supervision of China, the supervisory website of the Central Commission for Organization (the '12380' website), the reporting center of the Supreme People's Procuratorate, the reporting website of the Supreme People's Court, and the reporting mailbox of the Ministry of Land and Natural Resources.

4. Exercising power in a transparent manner

Just as sunshine is the best antiseptic, transparency is the best way to supervise power. Since the 1980s, the Chinese government has proactively implemented many systems to publicize government affairs, factory affairs, village affairs, as well as management of public enterprises and institutions. The *Regulations of the PRC on Publicizing Government Information* and some other important statutory documents have been promulgated. The regulations stipulate that government information that is not related to state secrets, business secrets or personal privacy should be made public in a timely and accurate manner, reflected by the requirement that government information that does not need to be dealt with very cautiously should be made public, so people's right to know, participate, express and supervise can be ensured. The party, state organs and governments at provincial levels (including autonomous regions and municipalities directly under the central government) have all established news release systems and spokesperson systems. Most governments above county level have established government websites. The state judicial organs have established an open system for administration of judicial affairs to ensure that court, procuratorial, police and prison affairs can be made known to the public, offering a strong guarantee for strengthening supervision over judicial activities. The CPC actively makes party affairs public through promulgating and implementing *The Opinions on Making Party Affairs Public at Grassroots Organizations*, improving the reporting mechanism for handling party affairs, promptly announcing party affairs, in particular important decisions made by party committees, selection and appointment of party cadres and the implementation of stipulations on combating corruption and self-discipline measures by leading party cadres, thus expanding the channels for CPC members to be informed about intra-party affairs and express their opinions. The Third Plenary Session of the 18th CPC Central Committee requires that we should improve the systems for publicizing party affairs, political affairs and affairs in other areas, and promote the transparency of decision-making, management, service delivery and the release of results after decisions are made.

5. Bribery crime archives

Bribery crime archives are categorized, recorded, and managed with computers by supervisory organs to prevent such crimes and improve the social trust system. They mainly include bribery in the fields of construction, finance, medicine and health, education and government procurement and are committed by individuals or organizations either providing or receiving bribes, or bribing go-betweens.

On February 16, 2012, an online bribery crime archive search system called the Bribery Blacklist was made available nationwide. Supervisory organs at all levels are able to search information on the internet about all bribery crimes throughout China. Any individual or organization with any bribery record will be disqualified from taking part in any engineering bidding or government procurement within a certain number of years. This system will be a huge help to prevent corruption.

6. Supervision over top leaders

Leading cadres face more temptations, and once they become corrupt, they can cause huge damage, for they hold more power. Therefore, China is dedicated to strengthening supervision over leading cadres, especially the top leaders, to prevent them from influence peddling. Democratic centralism, work reports and non-corruption reports, persuasion and admonition systems should be strictly carried out. The systems of accountability, promise of clean governance, administrative law enforcement responsibility, and responsibility of financial auditing for party and government leaders should all be monitored. The *CPC Guidelines for Leading Party Cadres to Perform their Official Duties with Integrity* should be put in place to improve the system of leading cadres reporting on personal matters. The supervision and accountability systems for selection and appointment of party cadres should be improved to strengthen the supervision over nomination, investigation and decision-making of party cadre selection and appointment. No privileged treatment or behavior is permissible. The *Plan for Establishing and Improving the Work of Punishing and Preventing Corruption (2013-2017)* issued by the CPC Central Committee stipulates that the pilot system of newly appointed cadres reporting on personal matters will be advanced, and regulations on strengthening management of the appointment of state functionaries whose spouses have emigrated will be formulated.

China has achieved great progress in its anti-corruption campaign after strenuous efforts to systematically control and comprehensively combat corruption. According to a public opinion poll conducted by the National Bureau of Statistics, people's satisfaction level regarding the anti-graft campaign rose from 51.9% in 2003 to 70.6% in 2010. In 2003, 68.1% of people considered corruption had been controlled; while in 2010, this figure had risen to 83.8%. The international community also gives China credit for this.

At the same time, we should be aware that the situation in combating corruption is still very serious, and the tasks are still formidable. As dramatic changes have been taking place in China's economic system, social structure, the pattern of interests, people's ideas and concepts, and various social problems have increasingly surfaced. Since relevant mechanisms and systems remain incomplete, bribery is still common in some fields. Some cases have become a bad influence in our society. Some prominent problems reported by the public are still not handled effectively. New problems keep cropping up in the process of improving the party's work style, upholding integrity and combating corruption. The types, features and means of committing crimes of bribery are undergoing new changes. The anti-corruption campaign is facing a complicated situation. First, remarkable results are being achieved while problems are still prominent. Second, more actions have been taken to prevent corruption while the number of corruption cases are increasing. Third, while people are expecting more from the government to fight corruption, it is hard to eradicate the problem in a short period of time.

We must thus make unremitting efforts to combat corruption, promote integrity and stay vigilant against degeneracy. The CPC and the Chinese government are always fully aware that it will be a protracted, complicated and arduous battle to fight against corruption. They will attach greater importance to combating corruption. They will resolutely punish and effectively prevent corruption with more confidence and resolution, and with powerful methods. All corruption must be dealt with and uprooted until there is no place left for it to exist, so as to win people's confidence with solid achievements in the anti-corruption campaign.

Chapter 8

How Does the CPC Pool the Strength of All Walks of Life for National Development?

The basic requirement for the development of a political party is to motivate and integrate social forces as much as possible through proper guidelines and practice. In other words, a political party should at least be capable of winning the support of, and pooling the wisdom and strength of, the people. The CPC, with fewer than 60 founding members at the beginning, has now become a political party boasting more than 88 million members, leading 1.3 billion people towards socialism with Chinese characteristics. One important reason for its success is that the CPC is capable of formulating and carrying out correct guidelines, principles and policies, and is able to pool the strength of all quarters and focus it on national development for the renaissance and common struggle of the Chinese nation through powerful theoretical and political work.

Members of China's 56 minority communities gathered at Potala Palace on September 27, 2012 to celebrate the 22nd 'Nationality Unity Month' and the first 'National Unity Progress Festival' in Lhasa (Jueguo, Xinhua News Agency)

Chapter 8

I. Stick to Fairness and Justice, and Take a Holistic Approach

The fundamental concept of the CPC in pooling the strength of all quarters is sticking to fairness and justice and taking a holistic approach. Fairness and justice are inherent requirements of socialism, and the primary value of a socialist system. To ensure social fairness and justice has always been the political ideology of CPC members. Back in those most arduous days, Mao Zedong said: "The affairs of a state are relevant to the whole nation. They are not the private affairs of a single party or group. Hence we communists have the duty to cooperate democratically with non-party people and have no right to exclude them and monopolize everything. The communist party is a political party which works in the interests of the nation and people and which has absolutely no private ends to pursue." China's reform and opening up has blazed a new trail for building socialism with Chinese characteristics. This historical process has also witnessed the CPC's efforts to ensure fairness and justice.

During China's reform and opening-up drive, Deng Xiaoping emphasized several times the importance of placing equal emphasis on material, ethical and cultural progress with no aspects being neglected. He said: "We should do two types of work at the same time: carrying out the policies of reform and opening up, and cracking down on economic crimes, including ideological and political work." The CPC proposed the important thought of Three Represents based on the changing situation of China and the whole world, which is undoubtedly connected with the CPC's political concept of fairness and justice. For the CPC, fairness and justice is not an empty slogan, but what should be carried out to develop advanced productive forces, to enhance advanced culture, and to uphold the fundamental interests of the overwhelming majority of the people. Fundamentally speaking, only when the thought of Three Represents is fully carried out can fairness and justice be realized in the CPC's governance and the majority of people be gathered together to fight for common goals and ideas.

In the new century, and despite the great results it has achieved in socialism, the CPC is fully aware of the existing problems in the process of development, especially the issue of uneven development. To deal with that, the concept of a Scientific Outlook on Development has been proposed in a timely manner. The top priority of the Scientific Outlook on Development is development. In this concept, people should be put first with regard to achieving comprehensive, balanced and sustainable development through taking a holistic approach. According to its requirements, ensuring fairness and justice means harmonizing the interests of different social groups and properly handling problems among the people and other social problems.

The holistic approach is the fundamental principle and experience as well as the basic approach to harmonize the interests of all parties. It is an important historical experience in governance for China, a developing country with more than a billion people. It is a significant strategy to be followed by the party in dealing with all types of problems. It is also a scientific and effective approach that the party has long adhered to. First of all, it is of great importance to understand the present interests and problems before following a holistic approach. China is still in the primary stage of socialism and will long remain so. This basic condition of China has not changed; nor has the principal problem in our society – how to meet the ever-growing material and cultural needs of the people with backward social production. In order to solve this problem and protect the fundamental interests of the overwhelming majority of the people, the first thing to do is to develop.

However, development alone is not enough. In the process of development, the fundamental interests of the overwhelming majority of people should be properly protected and ensured. Only when people are able to develop freely and comprehensively can social development be said to be fair and impartial. Meanwhile, only with comprehensive, balanced and sustainable development through a holistic approach can fairness and justice be represented to the greatest degree in the process and goals of economic and social development.

II. Properly Handle Every Type of Social Contradiction

After taking power, the CPC was confronted with various challenges and difficulties, among which social problems were persistent. In this process, CPC members remodeled governance ideas through creatively using the Marxist theory of social problems based on China's reality so as to fully understand the various problems and characteristics in its social development. Therefore, those social problems and conflicts have been handled properly, and problems in revolution, construction and reform are also being properly solved, so that comprehensive and balanced development in the economy, politics, culture, and society can be achieved, and experience in solving social problems and governing a country is gained.

First, maintaining the mass line is an important approach for the CPC to effectively solve social problems. Back in the times of war and revolution, the mass line was a powerful instrument for the CPC to conquer the enemy through mobilizing and organizing people. It was with the help of workers, farmers, soldiers, and intellectuals that the CPC finally won and became the ruling party. Now, in peacetime, the mass line is the best embodiment of the party's fundamental principle, which can help prevent corruption effectively. When solving social problems, the mass line requires the party and government to uphold this fundamental purpose, to listen to the opinions and requirements of the people, to understand the public mood, to conduct in-depth research among people, and to get first-hand information instead of acting upon assumptions. In the critical moment of social development, only by being of one mind with the people, sharing a common destiny with them, and understanding their real feelings and difficulties can the party help solve their problems, prove that the people's interests matter, solve the problems and harmonize the relationship between the party and the people and between cadres and the people. By doing so, the party can also make full use of the advantages of civil organizations and mass organizations to nip emerging problems in the bud quickly and accurately, so as to avoid them developing into huge problems endangering the whole country, or even changing their nature. That's how the mass line can alleviate social problems.

Second, putting the people first is the basic principle for effectively solving social problems. The Scientific Outlook on Development emphasizes putting people first and taking a holistic approach. Putting people first requires that the party must always make realizing, safeguarding and developing the fundamental interests of the overwhelming majority of the people the starting point and goal of all the work of the party and country, so as to protect people's rights and interests and to promote all-round development of the people. Adhering to a holistic approach requires that the party plays its role in exercising overall leadership, acting according to the overall plan, giving priority to the major work concerning the whole situation, and solving prominent problems related to people's interests. By adhering to these thoughts, we can solve various social problems and realize the goals of scientific development.

Third, following the principles of socialist democracy and rule by law is another approach to effectively solve social problems. Since the reform and opening up, especially since the establishment of a socialist market economy, interested parties have been diversified as a result of increasingly diverse economic sectors, and diverse interests have become more complicated, leading to more social problems in more complicated situations. It is getting more and more difficult to manage them only with rule by man. Therefore, the CPC proposed the basic strategy of law-based governance to accelerate the establishment and improvement of the legal system, and to build a legal framework suitable for a socialist market economy so as to regulate the behavior of all interested parties. With the help of systematization and law, the greediness of powerful groups can be suppressed, the interests they have access to can be limited, the social benefits of vulnerable groups can be secured, the pursuits of different walks of life can be considered, and a mechanism for the expression of multiple interests can be set up. Through this mechanism, all walks of life can negotiate and produce a concept of justice that is relatively approved by all. By improving people's awareness of law through education, a strict and incorruptible law enforcement team can be built to strictly punish corruption, so that the law can be resorted to when solving social problems.

Fourth, arming people with core socialist values is an effective cultural approach to solving social problems. Social problems come from economic and social issues, as well as from cultural factors, to a large degree. In order to solve those problems, we should highlight the themes of the times and arm people with core socialist values. We should foster a common ideal for socialism with Chinese characteristics and uphold socialist ethics. We should promote a culture of harmony, and pursue values of harmony. We should emphasize the concepts of 'harmonious but different' and 'harmony is the most precious'. We should encourage people to respect each other, trust each other and help each other. We should propel society to foster an environment of 'all for one and one for all'. We should guide members of society to be more positive and enterprising, and to strengthen their awareness of showing respect to others. Therefore, a good cultural environment can be created to solve social problems in an effective manner. It can serve as an ethical driving force to solve problems and enhance social harmony.

III. Create and Perfect a Mechanism to Coordinate Interests

A scientific interests coordinating mechanism can help to effectively resolve social interest conflicts, to promote innovation of social management and to maintain social harmony and stability. The party aims to build and improve such a mechanism.

First, efforts should be made to establish a mechanism for expressing people's opinions on benefits distribution. With the deepening of China's reform and the development of a socialist market economy, there are more diversified social interest groups, each expressing different opinions for profit distribution. Public policy makers should bear in mind the necessity to coordinate the relationship between interest groups or social classes. Due to the current reality, a mechanism in this regard should be formulated so that all social groups, especially vulnerable groups, have the opportunity to make demands, express opinions and offer suggestions via mechanisms designed for them. Such mechanisms will therefore be able to integrate and coordinate their social interests and promote social harmony and stability. The CPC has established several institutional platforms for the masses to express their interest requests, including institutions that require: leading cadres to receive people cordially; party and administrative leaders, party representatives, NPC representatives and CPPCC members to keep close ties with the people; a complaint letters and calls system; an information disclosure system; a system of hearings; a bargaining and negotiating system; and referendums. These are all basic systems that actively facilitate people in expressing their interest requests.

Second, efforts should be made to establish a fair and impartial mechanism for distribution of interests as the basic principle for coordinating the social interests of all parties. At first, the leading role of distribution according to work should be underscored, and the proportion of labor reward in the preliminary distribution be advanced to prevent capital profit from taking up too high a proportion of the revenue and match the reward with the amount of work. Then, the mechanism of collective salary negotiation should be established. With information imbalance and infrastructure investment as the main drivers of economic growth, capital still dominates while scattered labor forces are still in a disadvantageous and passive position. Therefore, a large amount of profits are more often taken by capital holders in proportion to the total distribution. In order to change the current situation, efforts should be made to improve relevant laws, and the mechanism of collective salary negotiation should be made compulsory instead of optional. A regular mechanism of wage increases should be established. The increase in workers' overall salary and average salary in an enterprise should not fall behind the increase in the enterprise's total profit. We must make sure that workers can share in the fruits of their company's development and that their wages and allowances increase in accordance with the company's improved production and profits.

Third, efforts should be made to establish a holistic mechanism for coordinating and adjusting various types of interests. The gap between rich and poor is inevitable in a market economy due to differences in terms of resource allocation, the natural environment and the invisible hand of the market. Therefore, the government should play its role as a visible hand to strengthen macro control and to coordinate the interests of developed areas and developing ones, between urban and rural areas, between monopoly and non-monopoly industries, and between the individual, the collective and the state. Efforts should be made to balance the interests of all parties and to promote common prosperity. At first, development in different regions, and in urban and rural areas should be coordinated. Tax, financial and fiscal policies should favor the support and development of developing and rural areas. A long-term mechanism for promoting the development of agriculture together with industry, developing as well as developed areas, and cities together with counties should be formulated. The most important thing is that overall regional fund allocation should be increased to support developing areas, especially in the countryside. The government strives to ensure that all the people share the achievements of reform and development by enhancing innovation in policies on public education, public health, full employment, fighting poverty and equalizing public services. Second, further efforts should be made to improve income distribution via taxation. Tax system reform should be deepened to make scientific and reasonable tax policy. The gap between rich and poor can be narrowed, and over-expansion of high-income groups' revenues can be curbed by charging graduated rates for taxes such as income tax, property tax and inheritance tax. Third, a social security system should be established. Efforts should be made to improve the social security system featuring social insurance, social welfare and social relief, and in particular to gradually expand the coverage of the system. Meanwhile, a scientific and reasonable benefit compensation system should be created. In the course of socialist modernization, land acquisition, house demolition and relocation of residents for construction are inevitable and will damage the interests of certain individuals and groups. It is necessary to establish a scientific and reasonable benefit compensation system based on these different cases that can reduce negative factors affecting social stability and promote society's harmonious and stable development. Last but not least, China's charities should be advanced energetically. Efforts should be made to foster charitable organizations, build charitable teams, develop various charitable assistance projects and give full play to the role of charitable organizations in relieving groups in need.

IV. Consolidate and Develop the Broadest Possible Patriotic United Front

United fronts are always important instruments for promoting the cause of the CPC and the people, and are used by the CPC to rule and rejuvenate the country. Under the leadership of the CPC, efforts should be made to develop the broadest possible patriotic united front that unites all democratic parties, people's organizations, nationalities, social strata and patriotic democrats. It is necessary for advancing the cause of the party and people. The work of various political organizations and a patriotic united front will contribute to mobilizing all positive forces and uniting all the forces that can be united so that everyone involved can work in harmony to maintain and strengthen political stability and unity in China. The work will also transform all negative forces into positive ones, promote social solidarity and harmony, and improve the party's social cohesion.

The CPC has always actively responded to the call of the times, following the aspirations of the people and integrating Marxist political theory and united front theory with China's reality. It has also created a socialist political system of multiparty cooperation and political consultation under the leadership of the CPC, has formed the broadest united front and taken the socialist path of making political advances with Chinese characteristics. The system of multiparty cooperation and political consultation under the leadership of the CPC is the basic political system of China. The CPC is the governing party, and multiparty cooperation must be carried out under the leadership of the CPC; non-CPC parties are political parties participating in the discussion and management of state affairs, and multiparty cooperation should give full play to and strengthen the role of non-CPC parties in participating in and supervising state affairs. The basic political system of China has its salient features and advantages. The CPC leads and all the other parties cooperate. The CPC governs and all the other parties participate in governance. Non-CPC parties are neither parties out of power nor opposition parties. They are friendly parties working closely with the CPC and participating in government. The CPC and non-CPC parties all carry out democratic consultation on major issues together, supervise each other and jointly improve the governance of the CPC and strengthen the participation of non-CPC parties in state affairs. Non-CPC parties are involved in a wide range of areas, including state power, consultation on state policies and candidates for state leaders, management of state affairs and formulation and implementation of state principles, policies, laws and regulations. At a new stage in a new century, based on a solid foundation, the practice of multiparty cooperation and political consultation under the leadership of the CPC will involve more issues in various areas.

First, the CPC is improving the system of carrying out consultations before major decisions are made. According to the *Opinions on Sticking to and Improving the System of Multiparty Cooperation and Political Consultation under the Leadership of the CPC*, non-CPC parties can take part in consultations in two ways. The first way is to consult with the CPC. For example, top leaders of the CPC Central Committee invite leaders of democratic parties to attend democratic consultation conferences; top leaders of the CPC Central Committee hold high-level, narrow-focus talks with leaders of non-CPC parties and public figures without party affiliation to exchange views and ideas as the situation requires; the CPC Central Committee convenes seminars participated in by democratic parties and representative figures without party affiliation. The second way is holding consultations at the CPPCC, which mainly focuses on the consultations before making decisions as well as on the process of implementing the decisions on major state and local policies, significant issues relating to politics, the economy, culture and social life. This form of political consultation is included in the decision-making process.

Second, the CPC is honest with and accepts supervision from non-CPC parties. To encourage non-CPC parties to conduct supervision, the CPC, on the basis of adhering to the Four Cardinal Principles, fully exercises democracy, solicits suggestions and proposals widely, encourages and supports non-CPC parties and public figures without party affiliation to offer opinions, criticisms and suggestions on the party's and state's principles and policies without reservation, and pays attention to their correct opinions. As the governing party, the CPC accepts supervision by non-CPC parties. This endeavor is helpful to reform and improves the decision-making process, enhances scientific and democratic decision-making, and better develops the party's lines, principles and policies. The CPC sees such opinions, criticisms and suggestions as motivation to make progress, as well as the basis on which to make decisions.

Third, the CPC is selecting more outstanding officials with no party affiliation to take up leading positions in government bodies at all levels. *Opinions on Sticking to and Improving the System of Multiparty Cooperation and Political Consultation Under the Leadership of the CPC* stipulates: on the issue of selecting and recommending officials with no party affiliation, there should be a proper proportion of non-CPC party members and public figures without party affiliation among NPC members, in the NPC Standing Committee and the NPC Special Committee; non-CPC party members and public figures without party affiliation should be selected as leaders of the State Council, and in ministries, local governments and their related departments; they should be recommended to take up leading positions in judicial and procuratorial bodies; they should also account for a proper proportion of leaders of the special committee of the CPPCC and the CPPCC's working organs. After certain improvement, the party will further train officials with no party affiliation, broaden the channels for their election and refine the way of using them, so as to further improve the selection system.

V. Properly Handle Relations with Union, Youth and Women's Organizations

Trade Unions, the Communist Youth League (CYL) and women's federations (hereafter referred to as union, youth and women's organizations) serve as the bridge between government and the people. And the CYL is the party's assistant and reserve force. During wartime and in the cause of socialist development and revolution, union, youth and women's organizations all played a significant role and gradually became administrative agencies of various regions, departments and institutions. Their primary jobs were supporting and implementing various principles and policies of the party and government, and undertaking work in the regions, departments and institutions that they were responsible for. In the new historical circumstances, the CPC is developing its relationships with union, youth and women's organizations in three ways.

First, the CPC supports union, youth and women's organizations to work independently under the party's leadership. The CPC is the faithful representative of the interests of all China's ethnic groups, as well as the leading core of the socialist cause. Sticking to the party's leadership is the cornerstone of achieving healthy growth of union, youth and women's organizations. Meanwhile, as mass organizations with a different nature and functions from party organizations, they are not functional departments of the party and can work independently according to the law and their own regulations. The party is strengthening and improving its role in leading them to work more actively and efficiently. Party committees make sure that they follow closely the party's guidelines in major decision-making while encouraging them to be active and innovative in specific tasks. Party organizations should never arrange everything for them or let them act totally on their own.

Second, the CPC makes sure that the union, youth and women's organizations properly deal with the relations between overall interests and specific interests. In a socialist society, people's fundamental interests are the same. But union, youth and women's organizations have their own specific interests and requirements, and sometimes their specific interests may be contradictory to the overall interests. Specific interests lose the basis of their existence if there are no overall interests, while if specific interests are not well taken care of, people become less motivated, which ultimately affects the overall interests. Therefore, the union, youth and women's organizations protect their own interests on the premise that the overall interests always assume priority. When specific interests contradict overall interests, the party directs people to put overall interests before individual, immediate and local interests. This is a basic principle to balance various interests in the new historical period.

Third, the CPC strikes a balance between the common features and the special features of the work union, youth and women's organizations. As mass organizations under the leadership of the CPC, union, youth and women's organizations have a lot in common. Meanwhile, as social organizations with a different nature, history, working staff and social functions, they have their own salient features and advantages. When giving instructions, the party pays attention to the common features of their work while, at the same time, fully considering their differences, and gives each of them specific instructions so as to give full play to their own advantages.

The CPC has always adhered to the mass line and paid attention to people's opinions. It has a firm grasp on ruling power, holds a strong belief in socialism, and gives full play to the role of union, youth and women's organizations. The party unites all the people to jointly overcome all difficulties so as to build socialism with Chinese characteristics.

Since the Reform and Opening-up program started, various social organizations have emerged, including professional associations, academic organizations, charities, funds, environmental protection organizations and cultural, sports and health organizations. The professional associations and academic organizations among them focus on industry, agriculture, science and technology, history, culture, philosophy and social sciences, and they have greatly pushed the development of academia and technology. Meanwhile, funds, charities and environmental protection organizations have made great contributions to protecting the environment and preventing environmental pollution and ecological deterioration. Various cultural, sports and health organizations have played a significant role in enriching people's lives and improving people's education level and health. Such emerging organizations are different from union, youth and women's organizations since they are all unofficial and organized spontaneously with no higher authorities leading them. They basically do not belong to the existing social management system, which poses new problems and challenges. To strengthen the management of social and non-governmental organizations, the party has issued the *Social Organizations Law* and made it clear that the registration and annual inspection of those organizations should be done by civil administration departments at various levels. Besides, the Federation of Social Science Workers has been set up in many provinces, municipalities, and autonomous regions, responsible for connecting and directing various relevant societies. As with the existing organization – the National Science Workers Association – it is also an administrative organ with budgeted posts and has set up party organizations. As for some small-scale and non-traditional social organizations, the party organizations at all levels communicate with them actively, convey the party's guidelines to them and encourage them to make contributions to the country and society, and benefit more people. The small-scale and non-traditional social organizations can also establish and develop party organizations. Relevant departments of government at all levels regulate them and their activities, making sure that they establish, develop and carry out activities according to the law. If some organizations display unhealthy development tendencies, necessary measures are immediately taken to prevent problems and rectify the situation.

Chapter 9

What is the Relationship Between the CPC and China's Military Power

"Control of the military determines whether a country prospers or declines,"[27] according to an old saying. Back in imperial times, armies were controlled as the ruling tools for the emperors, the slave owners and the landlords to protect their own interests and consolidate their rule. Now in a period when a party governs, the governing party, as the core of a country's political life, has the power to lead and manage the country, and therefore it must command and control the military through certain ways. That is to say, the military is a part of state power, as well as the military organizations for the ruling class. This is true for both capitalist and socialist countries.

The CPC develops its relationship with China's military power in accordance with the basic laws of political development. Meanwhile, this relationship has its own salient features: the party has definite power over the military, so as to maintain the advanced nature of the military and better provide military support for the cause of socialism.

I. Origin of the People's Liberation Army

Chinese revolution must take the road of armed struggle. The form of a country's revolutionary struggle and the road it takes depend on the conditions of the country. The New Democratic Revolution under the leadership of the CPC happened when China was a semi-colonial and semi-feudal country. It was a period when China was experiencing a special historical development, economic base and political structure, with the salient feature that imperialism, feudalism and bureaucrat-capitalism were oppressing the Chinese people. After the Xinhai Revolution in 1911 raised the concept

---

[27] Fan Jun (the Southern Song Dynasty): *Of the Five Dynasties*

of establishing a bourgeois-democratic republic, China was still in a semi-colonial and semi-feudal state and its people still lived under oppression. And to make things even worse, warlords came onto the stage and drove China into turmoil. They ruled over different regions and initiated constant wars, which caused great misery to the Chinese people. Under such a reactionary ruling class, China had no national independence because of imperialism, and had no democracy because of feudalism. Therefore, legal revolutionary struggle was not allowed and unlikely to be carried out in such a state without a parliamentary system. The aim of China's revolution was to overthrow imperialism, feudalism and bureaucrat-capitalism, so as to achieve national independence and liberate the people. The target of the revolution was the fully armed reactionary ruling class, which was powerful and stubborn, and would never give up easily. All those facts showed that China, unlike European capitalist countries, was not able to take the road of parliamentary battle. Its basic conditions determined that the major form of revolution would be war. When the CPC was founded, there was a discussion about violent revolution. However, China did not take the road of armed struggle until the National Revolution (1924-1927) had failed. At a conference held by the CPC Central Committee on August 7, 1927, Mao Zedong stated: "We must pay special attention to military power in the future. Political power grows out of the barrel of a gun."[28] He later reflected on the experiences of China's revolution: "The seizure of power by armed force, the settlement of the issue by war, is the central task and the highest form of revolution." He went on to say: "Without armed struggle, neither the proletariat and the people, nor the CPC would have had any standing at all in China and it would have been impossible for the revolution to triumph."[29] The Chinese Communists represented by Mao Zedong, according to the basic conditions of China, carried out guerrilla warfare in rural areas where the enemy's rule was weak, built rural bases and seized the countryside to encircle and finally capture the cities. This was a revolutionary course with Chinese characteristics, a further development of Marxism, and a correct choice based on China's reality.

To carry out armed struggle, an army led by the CPC had to be established. The special conditions of China determined that armed struggle had to be carried out throughout the course of China's revolution. And to carry out such armed struggle, there had to be armies led by the CPC. The guidelines made at the First National Congress of the CPC in 1921 when

---
[28] *Collected Works of Mao Zedong*, Vol. I, Beijing People's Publishing House, 1993, page 47
[29] *Collected Works of Mao Zedong*, Vol. II, Beijing: People's Publishing House, 1993, pages 541 & 544

the CPC was officially established stipulated that the CPC should overthrow the bourgeoisie by proletarian armed force. However, from 1921 to 1927 when the National Revolution failed, the CPC did not have its own armies. The establishment of the CPC's armies later was, to some extent, driven by KMT reactionaries. In 1925 when the CPC and KMT were cooperating, the KMT established its own armed force – the National Revolutionary Army – by imitating the Soviet Union's military system. In July 1926, the Northern Expedition (1926-1927) burst out and the two parties went from one victory to another. However, the Nationalist Chiang Kai-shek stole the leadership of the Northern Expedition and expanded the military force of the KMT. What is worse, he colluded with both Chinese and foreign reactionaries and massacred the Communists and the revolutionary masses. On April 12, 1927, the military forces of Chiang Kai-shek initiated the Shanghai massacre and by July 15, 1927, the Wuhan regime had also expelled the communists in its ranks. Those two incidents killed thousands of unarmed communists and major figures in the peasants' and workers' movements, ending the cooperation between the KMT and the CPC. The National Army built up by the KMT reactionaries led by Chiang Kai-shek during the Northern Expedition became new warlord troops and a tool of the reactionary KMT ruler. The party, sobered up by the lessons paid for with blood, realized that without an army controlled exclusively by the CPC, the Chinese people could not be truly liberated. Though small victories could have been won, crushing defeat was waiting. Oppressed and frustrated, the people also felt that without a people's army, their rights and interests could not have been realized and protected, and they could have lost their lives any minute. As Mao Zedong said: "It is the whole nation's obligation to build a people's army. The Chinese people can achieve nothing without the support of a people's army. As for this issue, actions speak louder than words."[30] On August 7, 1927, the CPC Central Committee held an emergency meeting in Hankou (also known as the August 7 Meeting). The meeting corrected the mistaken concept of Chen Duxiu, the leader of the CPC, "who never thought of arming the peasants and workers and the importance of doing it and did not consider building a peasants' and workers' army". The mission of arming the peasants and workers and building a revolutionary army was set out and "given top priority"[31] at the meeting. According to an order made by

---

[30] *Collected Works of Mao Zedong*, Vol. III, Beijing: People's Publishing House, 1993, page 1,074
[31] *CPC Central Committee Document Anthology*, Vol. III, Beijing: Central Party School Press, 1983, page 263

the CPC Central Committee, the Front Committee of the communist party led by Zhou Enlai staged the Nanchang Uprising, which was the prelude to actions against the KMT. Afterwards, the Autumn Harvest Uprising led by Mao Zedong and the Guangzhou Uprising led by Zhang Tailei took place, along with almost a hundred insurrections all over China. The CPC entered a new era where a people's army was taking shape and a revolutionary war under the party's independent leadership was raging.

An armed uprising in Nanchang, Jiangxi on October 1, 1927 marked the beginning of an independent arms struggle led by the CPC (Xinhua News Agency)

The Origin of the People's Liberation Army

The People's Liberation Army (PLA) was established on August 1, 1927 and led by the CPC. It originally went under the names of: the Second Army of the National Revolutionary Army, the Chinese Workers' and Peasants' Revolutionary Army, the Chinese Workers' and Peasants' Red Army, the Eighth Route Army, the New Fourth Army and the People's Liberation Army.

From the Chinese Workers' and Peasants' Revolutionary Army to the Chinese Workers' and Peasants' Red Army

On August 1, 1927, the Front Committee of the CPC led by Zhou Enlai and more than 20,000 soldiers led by He Long, Ye Ting, Zhu De and Liu Bocheng *initiated an armed uprising in Nanchang, known as the Nanchang Uprising. It was the first major KMT–CPC engagement of the Chinese Civil War, marking the beginning of the independent armed struggle against the KMT led by the CPC. On September 9, 1927, the peasants, workers and soldiers in the border areas of Hunan and Jiangxi Provinces initiated the Autumn Harvest Uprising under the leadership of Mao Zedong. The major armed forces engaged in this uprising were enrolled in the First Division, First Army of the Chinese Workers' and Peasants' Revolutionary Army. This was the first time that the Chinese Workers' and Peasants' Revolutionary Army was established and known by the public.*

In late April, 1928, Zhu De and Chen Yi led the remaining armed forces after the Nanchang Uprising joined forces with the Chinese Workers' and Peasants' Revolutionary Army under the leadership of Mao Zedong at the Jinggang Mountains. In this way, the Fourth Army of the Chinese Workers' and Peasants' Revolutionary Army was established with Zhu De as army commander, and Mao Zedong as party representative (later called commissar). On May 25, 1928, the CPC Central Committee issued the 51st notice, stipulating that the name of Chinese Workers' and Peasants' Revolutionary Army should be changed to the Chinese Workers' and Peasants' Red Army (the Red Army). From August 1930 to July 1936, three Red Armies were formed – the First Red Army, the Fourth Red Army and the Second Red Army. In May, the Red Army headquarters was established with Zhu De as commander-in-chief and Zhou Enlai as chief commissar.

From the Chinese Workers' and Peasants' Red Army to the Eighth Route Army and the New Fourth Army

After the Lugou Bridge Incident in 1937, the CPC struck a deal with the KMT. According to the deal, the main force of the Red Army was renamed the Eighth Route Army of the National Revolutionary Army or the 'Eighth Route Army' for short in August 1937. The army consisted of three divisions – the 115th, the 120th and the 129th – and one troop under direct command of the headquarters with Zhu De as commander-in-chief and Peng Dehuai, deputy commander-in-chief. The army numbered some 46,000 people. In September 1937, the Military Affairs Commission of the Nationalist Government ordered the Eighth Route Army to be renamed 'the 18th Army Group of the National Revolutionary Army', based in the 2nd War Zone. The commander-in-chief and deputy commander-in-chief remained unchanged. However, the name 'Eighth Route Army' had been widely accepted by the masses, so it was still used to refer to the army.

In October 1937, the CPC and KMT made an announcement that the guerrilla forces of the Red Army active in 15 regions in the eight provinces of Hunan, Jiangxi, Fujian, Guangdong, Zhejiang, Hubei, Henan and Anhui would form the New Fourth Army of the National Revolutionary Army, or the 'New Fourth Army' for short. Ye Ting was the army commander and Xiang Ying, the deputy army commander.

From the Eighth Route Army and the New Fourth Army to the People's Liberation Army

From the end of the War of Resistance against Japanese Aggression to June 1946, 27 field troops (or divisions) and 6 field brigades were formed with 610,000 brigaded soldiers in addition to 660,000 local soldiers. In June 1946, the KMT broke the Armistice Agreement signed with the CPC and launched massive attack on the Central Plains, hence, the full-scale civil war broke out. Soldiers and civilians in every liberated zone rose up and fought back, leading to the outbreak of People's Liberation War on a national scale. Due to the fundamental change of the strategic missions, the army led by the CPC was renamed "People's Liberation Army" in mid-September 1946. Zhu De was appointed the Commander-in-Chief and Peng Dehuai, the Deputy Commander-in-Chief. Then, the name "People's Liberation Army" has been used ever since.

II. The New Military Force

Although the army was controlled exclusively by the CPC, it still fell short of being a new people's army. To transform an army mainly composed of peasants and insurrectionary forces into an armed force capable of carrying out its revolutionary political mission, the CPC still had a long way to go. After the emergency meeting held by the CPC Central Committee on August 7, 1927, the new Politburo of the CPC further proposed the principle of establishing a revolutionary army on August 9, not by employing soldiers but by recruiting volunteers and gradually forming a workers' and peasants' army with a conscription system. The politburo also indicated that "the army of hired soldiers and local troops should be reorganized so as to develop a core force for the revolutionary army".[32]

During the early development of a people's army, many soldiers left the army and defeatism prevailed when the insurrectionary forces attacked

---

[32] *CPC Central Committee Document Anthology*, Vol. III, Beijing: Central Party School Press, 1983, page 291

Changsha and marched to the Jinggang Mountains. The army's manpower was greatly reduced. A state of total confusion had sapped morale. Mao Zedong keenly sensed the potential danger in the army structure and the system. So, upon marching towards the Jinggang Mountains, Mao reorganized the force in Sanwan Village, Yongxin County of Jiangxi Province, which is known historically as the 'Sanwan Reorganization'. The move formulated the principle of 'establishing party branches on a company basis'. In a company there is a party branch, with a party group in each squad and platoon. In the organizations above company level there was a party representative. In each battalion and regiment there was a party committee. The troops were all under the leadership of the Front Committee of the CPC. It was stipulated that officers should not beat soldiers; officers and soldiers should enjoy equal treatment; soldiers were free to voice their opinions in meetings; red tape was abolished; and accounts were made public. In order to guarantee the democratic rights of soldiers, soldier committees composed of representatives elected by soldiers were set up in organizations above company level to enable soldiers to take a hand in economic and administrative management. Thus a new relationship featuring unity between officers and soldiers was established. The Gutian Congress corrected mistaken party ideology such as non-proletarian thoughts and unsophisticated military viewpoints and set out the nature, aims and tasks of the Red Army. It drew a clear line between a new people's army and an old-fashioned one. It highlighted the political work within the Red Army and promoted a democratic system in the army. A new relationship featuring unity between officers and soldiers and between the army and the people was established. Hence, the construction of a people's army was put on the right track. Many years later, in retrospect, Mao Zedong said: "The principle of 'organizing the party branch on a company basis' was an important reason why the Red Army was able to carry on such arduous fighting without falling apart."[33] And "apart from the role played by the party, the reason why the Red Army was able to carry on in spite of such poor material conditions and frequent engagements was its practice of democracy." In his book *Mao: A Biography*, American writer Ross Terrill also noted that this principle "dissolved the party from an abstract concept into an everyday reality, and brought it to the campfire and to the hands that held the rifles".[34]

---

[33] *The Selected Works of Mao Zedong*. Vol. II. Beijing: People's Publishing House,1991, page 65-6
[34] Terrill, Ross. *Mao: A Biography*. Beijing: China Renmin University Press, 2006, page 263

Chapter 9

A painting of Mao Zedong speaking to the Workers and Peasants Red Army in Sanwan Village, Yongxin County, Jiangxi, on September 29, 1927. Here Mao Zedong carried out the 'Sanwan Reform' and established the principle of 'establishing party branches on a company basis' (Xinhua News Agency)

The Sanwan Reorganization entrenched the leadership position of the CPC over the army. Later on, the principle that 'the party commands the gun' was established during the rivalry between the separatist party led by Zhang Guotao and the Red Army. In 1935, a bitter disagreement between Zhang Guotao and Mao Zedong caused a split in the party and the Red Army. Zhang insisted that whoever had more guns should have more power and that it was the gun that commanded the party. The Central Committee stood firmly against his viewpoint. In the *Problems of War and Strategy* written on November 6, 1938, Mao Zedong gave his thoughts on the conflict: "Our principle is that the party commands the gun, and the gun must never be allowed to command the party."[35] Mao Zedong summed up the relationship between the party and the army from the aspect of political principle and for the first time formally presented the viewpoint as a principle that the party had absolute leadership over the army. After Japan launched its large-scale assault on China, the CPC had the Red Army incorporated into the National Revolutionary Army but was forced to hand over the armed forces and their military power to the KMT. Within the party, Wang Ming, from a rightist capitulationist standpoint, believed that a united national defense force should be set up. Mao Zedong sniped at Wang's wrong political views

---

[35] *Selected Works of Mao Zedong, Vol. III (M), Beijing: People's Publishing House, 1991, page 547*

and insisted that the CPC should maintain its independence from the united front in the Red Army and all the guerrilla forces. The CPC did not waver in this matter. The CPC also rejected the KMT's demand to appoint a KMT member to be a senior officer of the Eighth Route Army. The CPC restored the Political Commissar System and the name of the political department, which was once abolished due to intervention by the KMT, eventually smashing the KMT's plot to gobble up the armed forces. The party's insistence on retaining its absolute authority over the army led to a great leap in its control over military power, from individual leadership to party leadership. It completely ruled out the revival of stratocracy and extricated China from the nightmare where the party was manipulated by warlords.

III. The People's Military Force

The founding of the PRC marked the end of China's semi-colonial and semi-feudal state and ushered the country into a new era. As the CPC rose to become the ruling power, the people's army naturally became the state's military force. As a result, the army aborted its original mission of overthrowing the reactionary rule of the KMT and seizing political power, and took on the mission of consolidating national defense, resisting aggression, defending sovereignty, safeguarding people's lives, joining in national construction and serving the people wholeheartedly.

1. China's military forces are the military forces of the socialist state

"The state is a product and a manifestation of the irreconcilability of class antagonisms." A state, in essence, is a tool for one class to rule other classes. Whoever wants to achieve and maintain dominance must make the best use of the tool. The army, prisons, courts and various enforcement agencies are important components of state power and instruments with which the state's will is implemented, the nature of the state is kept and the state's power is cemented. From the perspective of building a socialist country, the very nature of a people's army under the party's leadership being a military force of the state is embodied in the military leadership system.

In September 1949, the *Common Program of the CPPCC (Common Program)* was adopted as a temporary constitution by the First Plenary Session of the CPPCC. The *Common Program* stipulated that leading military organs should be included in the political regime. It read: "The armed forces of the

PRC, namely, the PLA, the people's public security forces and the people's police belong to the people." The PRC will build a unified army, namely the PLA, and people's public security forces, which will be under the command of the People's Revolutionary Military Commission of the Central People's Government."[36] The establishment of the People's Revolutionary Military Commission was a signal that the leading military organs under the CPC had been officially incorporated into the country's political regime.

The First Plenary Session of the First National People's Congress held in 1954 decided to set up the National Defense Commission of the PRC and the Ministry of National Defense of the PRC and invalidate the Commander-in-Chief of the PLA. The *Constitution of the PRC* adopted at the meeting stipulated that: "The armed forces of the PRC belong to the people; their duty is to safeguard the gains of the people's revolution and the achievements of national construction, and to defend the sovereignty, territorial integrity and security of the state," and "The Chairman of the PRC commands the state's armed forces and is Chairman of the National Defense Council."[37] In a bid to strengthen the party's authority over the army, the Political Bureau of the CPC Central Committee adopted the *Resolution on the Establishment of the Central Military Commission of the CPC* on September 28, 1954. The resolution stated that the CPC military commission should be placed under the leadership of the Politburo and the CPC Secretariat as before and should assume the command of military work.[38]

The 1982 Constitution provided an institutional basis for the PRC Central Military Commission leadership system. The *PRC Constitution* adopted at the Fifth Plenary Session of the Fifth National People's Congress stipulated that "the armed forces of the PRC belong to the people. The Central Military Commission of the PRC controls the country's armed forces. The chairman assumes overall responsibility for the work of the Central Military Commission. The chairman and members of the Central Military Commission of the PRC, upon nomination by the CPC, are elected by the National People's Congress. The term of office of the Central Military Commission is the same as that of the National People's Congress." The establishment of the Central Military Commission marked a significant change of the country's political and military system in a new historical stage.

---

[36] *Anthology of Important Literature Since the Founding of the PRC*, Vol. I, Beijing: Central Party Literature Press, 1992, page 6
[37] *Anthology of Important Literature Since the Founding of the PRC*, Vol. V, Beijing: Central Party Literature Press, 1992, page 531
[38] Party History Research Center of the CPC Central Committee: *Chronicle of the Communist Party of China,* Beijing: Communist Party of China History Publishing House, 2006,

The Central Military Commission of the CPC and the Central Military Commission of the PRC were blended into one, with the same staff, leading organs and functions. The mandates that the two military commissions gave to the PLA were implemented by the General Staff Department, the General Political Department, the General Logistics Department and the General Armament Department within the Central Military Commission of the PRC. In the meantime, the Ministry of National Defense of the PRC was established under the State Council. It exercises administration over the government's military work after the State Council has given its instructions. The Ministry of National Defense is headed by the State Council and is also subordinate to the Central Military Commission of the PRC. This leadership system clearly explains the status, functions, tasks and other important aspects of a people's army in serving a socialist country. The incorporation of the army into the country's organizational system defined by law ensures legal recognition of the PLA's position in the country's regime. This embodies and guarantees the CPC's absolute leadership over the PLA. Furthermore, it helps consolidate military development, promote the modernization of national defense, prepare the whole country for wartime if necessary, promote quicker response to emergencies, defend the country and ensure the steady progress of socialist construction. The great institutional achievements of the CPC in army building and management are also a significant sign of the advanced status of socialist development in China.

2. China's military forces are the Chinese people's military forces

The sole purpose of China's military forces is to wholeheartedly serve the people. The connection between the army and the people determines the relationship between the CPC and the army. The people's army safeguards Chinese people's interests. As the CPC represents the fundamental interests of the people, it puts the army in a better position to fulfill its objectives when the army is placed under the leadership of the party.

The people's army belongs to the people. During a period in the history of the Republic of China, warlord troops were mostly controlled by individuals or cliques, such as the Fengtian clique, Anhui clique, Ma clique and Chiang's Whampoa Clique. These armies, in essence, served the private interests of warlords by milking money from common people and contending for power. In September 1927, the Chinese Workers' and Peasants' Red Army emerged in the Autumn Harvest Uprising. In the

Sanwan Reorganization, Mao Zedong downsized a division to a regiment under the guideline of "stay or leave as you wish". Thus, an army of hired soldiers was turned into an army of volunteers. The concept of joining the army for the sake of money was discarded and a new belief of revolutionary soldiers fighting for the people was developed. In November 1928, Mao wrote in a report to the Central Committee of the CPC: "The Red Army has abolished the mercenary system, making the men feel they are fighting for themselves and for the people, not for somebody else."[39] The *Gutian Congress Resolution* adopted in December 1929 pointed out that the Red Army was an armed body for carrying out revolutionary political tasks. It was a means of accomplishing political tasks. It served the proletariat and the masses. "The Red Army should certainly not confine itself to fighting; besides fighting to destroy the enemy's military strength, it should shoulder important tasks such as doing propaganda among the masses, organizing the masses, arming them, helping them to establish revolutionary political power and setting up party organizations." "The Red Army fights not merely for the sake of fighting but to conduct propaganda among the masses, organize them, arm them, and help them to establish revolutionary political power. Without these objectives, fighting loses its meaning and the Red Army loses the reason for its existence."[40] The resolution elaborated on the relationship between the army and the masses and defined the nature, objectives and tasks of the people's army, laying a solid foundation for building a new people's army. This trait of the people's army left a strong impression on those who had had contact with the army. On July 22, 1944, the US Army General Headquarters in China sent its first group of observers to Yan'an. John Paton Davies, Junior, a member of the US Army Observation Group (or Dixie Mission), wrote in his report: "The CPC had gone through 10 years of civil war and seven years of the anti-Japanese war. They were subject to greater pressure than the army of the central government and the watertight blockade imposed by Chiang Kai-Shek." But they "survived and thrived". The sheer tenacity of the party can be attributed to the fact that "the government and army under the command of the CPC are widely supported by the masses. And the reason that the government and army had gained great popularity was that they belonged to the people."[41]

The people's army serves the people. The armed forces in countries

---

[39] *Selected Works of Mao Zedong*, Vol. I, Beijing: People's Publishing House, 1991, page 63
[40] Ibid. page 86
[41] Li Changjiu and Shi Lujia, *200 Years of Sino-US Relations,* Beijing: Xinhua Publishing House, 1984, page 116

ruled by the exploiting classes safeguard the interests of the rulers rather than those of the people. Established and led by the CPC, the Chinese armed forces were formed to liberate the people from exploitation. In 1944, Mao Zedong delivered a speech entitled 'Serve the People' in which he said: "Our army aims to liberate the people and serves completely the interests of the people."[42] In his report to the Seventh National Congress of the CPC in April 1945, Mao summarized the purpose of the people's army as follows: "Standing closely by the people while serving them wholeheartedly is the sole purpose of the army."[43] During the Chinese Civil War (1946-1949), Mao drafted a declaration for the PLA's headquarters in which he proclaimed: "This army is an army of the Chinese people and its will is decided by that of the people."[44] After the establishment of the PRC, the Constitution stipulated that the PRC's armed forces belong to the people and their tasks are to strengthen national defense, resist aggression, defend the motherland, safeguard the people's peaceful labor, participate in national reconstruction and do their best to serve the people.

The people's army loves the people. When the people's army was first established, Mao pointed out that the army had three tasks: carrying out military missions, raising funds and doing mass work. Strict discipline had to be maintained to complete these tasks. Therefore, during the Red Army's struggles against the KMT, Mao laid down several disciplinary matters that needed to be addressed, including caring about people's interests and respecting local CPC organizations and governments. In April 1928, he outlined these disciplines and noteworthy matters as 'Three Disciplines and Six Matters for Attention', which were later revised and updated to 'Three Disciplines and Eight Matters for Attention'. Embodying explicitly the nature of the new people's army, these norms of behavior became its common disciplines and traditions. According to *The Biography of Mao Zedong*, during that time "the lyrics of a popular ballad were 'the Red

Comrade LeiFeng, a model soldier of the 1960s, who devoted his life to serving the people (Xinhua News Agency)

---

[42] *The Selected works of Mao Zedong*, Vol. III, Beijing: People's Publishing House, 1991, page 1,004
[43] *The Selected Works of Mao Zedong*. Vol. III, Beijing: People's Publishing House, 1991, page 1,039
[44] *The Selected works of Mao Zedong*, Vol. IV, Beijing, People's Publishing House, 1991, page 1,237

Army follows discipline and orders, cares about us and wins our love, asks about our opinions, does business fairly and brings no harm to people's interests'. From then on, the relationship between the Red Army and the people changed. These norms of behavior laid an important foundation for the development of the Red Army and the victories against its enemies."[45]

At the threshold of the 21st century, Hu Jintao, former General Secretary of the CPC, stressed: "To fulfill its purpose of putting people first, the army must consistently adhere to its nature as a people's army and safeguard people's fundamental interests. Under the absolute leadership of the CPC, the PLA is from the people and for the people. Serving the people wholeheartedly is the sole aim and the highest principle of the army. The idea of standing by the people and for the people serves as an ideological foundation and a source of strength for the army to fight for victories."[46]

IV. Adhere to the CPC's Absolute Leadership over the Army

Adhering to the CPC's absolute leadership over the army is a truth learned by the CPC during its long struggles. It is the foundation of the army's establishment and the power for its development.

Adhering to the CPC's absolute leadership over the army was decided by China's modern history. Modern China has witnessed various political parties and organizations as well as all kinds of armies and armed forces. However, none of them managed to shoulder the responsibility of saving the nation from doom and striving for its survival and rejuvenation. Therefore all of them failed and were consigned to the past. Why did only the CPC manage to take that responsibility? One important reason lies in the fact that the CPC is an advanced party armed with Marxism and commands a loyal proletarian army. History has fully proved that upholding the CPC's absolute leadership over the army was an inevitable outcome of modern Chinese history and a wise choice made by the CPC and the people's army, and meets the intrinsic demand of the unique rules of the Chinese revolution.

Adhering to the CPC's absolute leadership over the army was also determined by the political system with Chinese characteristics. The establishment of the PRC began our path towards a socialist country under the people's democratic dictatorship led by the working class and based on the alliance of workers and peasants. Differing from the multiparty systems

---
[45] Jin Chongji: *The Biography of Mao Zedong,* Beijing: Central Literature Press, 1996
[46] Liu Yuan: The Position of the Gutian Conference in the History of Army Building, Qiushi Journal (16th edition in 2007)

of western countries, we adopted a system of multiparty cooperation and political consultation under the leadership of the CPC, which makes the CPC the core leader during China's socialist construction. Since the political system decides the military system, China's military forces should only be led and commanded by the CPC rather than by any other political power, which conforms well to the political system with Chinese characteristics. The CPC's absolute leadership over the army constitutes China's fundamental military system and an integral part of the socialist political system with Chinese characteristics.

Adhering to the CPC's absolute leadership over the army is a necessary choice to ensure China's enduring order and stability. The fate of a country varies according to who leads its army. China's modern history witnessed protracted wars between warlords, leaving the country defenseless when invaded by foreign countries. The cause of this was that the armies served as a tool for individuals and interest groups with narrow minds. Only the army led by the CPC never flinched from fighting for the country and the people, making itself a great power to defend the country and protect the people. Whenever the country and its people are in danger, this heroic and skillful army led by the CPC stands up and takes responsibility for protecting the people and stabilizing society and the country. Currently, faced with a complex environment and expanding national interests, we urgently need a harmonious and stable internal environment and a secure external environment to push forward the socialist modernization construction. Only with CPC leadership can the army loyally fulfill the sacred mission entrusted to it by the party and the people, serving as a powerful security guarantee for building a moderately prosperous society in all respects and for realizing China's enduring order and stability.

For more than 90 years, the CPC has managed to explore effective ways to guarantee its absolute leadership over the army. The nature of this leadership lies in leading the army with ideological and political work. When the CPC was founded in July 1921, opinions inside the party varied on whether to build an army under the leadership of the CPC or not and how to lead this army once established. Mao Zedong and other senior revolutionaries put forward the principle of 'cultivating the party on the ideological level' in a clear-cut manner and conducted unique political work in the army. It focused on the ideological and political education of the army by equipping soldiers with advanced political ideology and theories. After the Sanwan Reorganization, the party always educated its soldiers with revolutionary theories and the party's ideals and conviction to enable them to clearly envision the revolution's future. At the Gutian Conference, Mao clearly pointed out that the education problem needed to be solved urgently. During its subsequent revolutionary activities and party construction, the CPC always gave priority to building the army with ideological and political work. The party armed soldiers' minds with innovative theories and improved its ideological and political education by keeping up with the times, the mission and the soldiers' real needs, making soldiers deeply mindful of what 'the army's soul' is all about. History shows that the CPC's absolute leadership over the army in essence is leading the army with theoretical and political work. Faced with new challenges in the ideological and cultural sphere, we must focus on ideological and political education and establish the idea of 'loyalty to the party' as the cornerstone of modern revolutionary soldiers' core values; we must make it a fundamental job to equip soldiers with the party's innovative theories so as to enhance the ideological and political foundation for the CPC's leadership over the army; we must fight strongly against such wrong thoughts as 'the army should not be subordinate to the party', 'the army should not be politicized' or that 'the army should be nationalized', ensuring that soldiers stay closely in line with the CPC Central Committee and the Central Military Commission both ideologically and politically.

The key to achieving the CPC's absolute leadership over the army is to establish a scientific leadership system under which collective leadership over the army by party organizations at all levels can be achieved. In order to truly transfer the command of the army from an individual to a political party, the leadership system must stay in line with the realities of the party, the country and the army. For more than nine decades, the CPC has established a range of scientific leadership systems including the Party Committee System, the Political Commissar System and the Political Organization System, whose core element is the system of senior military officers assuming separate responsibilities under the collective leadership of the party committee. In addition, the CPC has set up elaborate rules and regulations to run the Party Congress of the army, Inner-Party Elections, Inner-Party Supervision, Requests for Instructions, meetings of democratic life and reporting on one's work and one's performance related with corruption and graft. Thanks to this scientific leadership system, the army grew from one consisting mainly of peasants and the petty bourgeoisie into a new people's army which kept in line with the party's political targets on all crucial occasions. History has repeatedly proved that it is completely correct and effective to adhere to the military leadership systems and principles with Chinese characteristics.

In the new period, apart from upholding this scientific system, we need to further innovate its specific content to keep up with the development of the party and the national political system, and improve the party's military leadership during wartime to adapt to the new features of regional warfare in the information age; we must also strengthen the legal and theoretical foundations for the party's absolute leadership over the army in response to the new requirements of the rule of law and governing the army by law.

Realization of the CPC's absolute leadership over the army must rely on people who are completely loyal to the party and politically trustworthy, to ensure that the highest leadership and command over the army are in the hands of the CPC Central Committee and the Central Military Commission. Such a requirement can be implied from the word 'absolute', which also means that the party is the only leading body of the army. For more than 90 years, the party has been fighting with hostile and reactionary forces for the army's leadership, which in fact is a scramble for talent. Therefore, the party sticks to the principle of cadres managed by the party and inspected by political organs, the purpose of which is to ensure that the power of selecting people is in the party's hands; the party always gives top priority to one's political performance when selecting people so as to guarantee that the selected cadres at all levels follow the party's words and orders; the party has always been working towards establishing and improving the cadre selection policies and regulations to achieve a normalized and scientific selection process. Over the years, our army has remained firm after major political struggles and other significant historic moments; it keeps united, strong, steadfast and politically correct when faced with severe dangers, obstacles and temptation from hostile forces. The reason behind all of this lies in the fact that the party has selected and cultivated many generals and commanders with clear minds, good political performance, great talent and achievements. It is also attributed to the fact that the party leads an army of cadres who are politically staunch, of strong military ability and good performance, and who thus constitute the backbone of the army. Faced with new circumstances and missions, we must steadfastly uphold the principle of the armed forces and cadres being governed by the party and keep improving the mechanism for selecting talent and giving full rein to their abilities, which helps attract capable people from various areas to work for the construction of the party and the army; we should hold fast to the selection standard of attaching importance to both professional competence and political integrity but giving priority to the latter, the purpose of which is to promote cadres who are politically reliable, capable at work, trusted by other soldiers and with high integrity to take on leading posts of different levels; we should unswervingly educate and govern cadres through ideological work, organizational structure, and rules and regulations in a strict manner to guarantee that the military leadership remains in the hands of Marxists who are loyal to the party.

Achieving the CPC's absolute leadership over the army also depends on strong leadership of party organs and the pioneering role of party cadres. The reason for this lies in the fact that party organs and party cadres take on the obligation of exercising command over the army. During the revolutionary wars, our army survived hundreds of battles and annihilated millions of enemies thanks to party organs and cadres in the army whose excellent command united all soldiers and boosted their morale. During the era of peaceful construction, the CPC continued focusing on enhancing its advanced nature and abilities in the process of economic, political, cultural, social and ecological construction (known as 'Five in One'). These efforts not only refine party organs and improve their leadership capabilities, but also purify party members and promote their overall qualities, helping them withstand tests and remain advanced. Since maintaining advanced and enhanced capabilities cannot be a one-off, we must keep clear minds and sharpen our senses to dangers and be eager for knowledge. Currently we must uphold arming the army with innovative theories as the core while strengthening understanding about party organizations and enhancing all party organs' capabilities, which include those of keeping politically correct in army building, taking a holistic approach in planning, leading the army in a scientific way, commanding the army to carry out multiple military missions and promoting the army's all-round development in a creative way; we should emphasize strengthening the army through ideological work and enhancing the cultivation of leaders and give full rein to the core leadership of party committees and the pioneering role of cadres, which is to guide soldiers to voluntarily defend the party's authority, follow the party's orders and complete tasks entrusted by the party; we should focus on carrying out activities to encourage CPC members and organizations to excel in their work while strengthening the construction of primary party organizations to intensify their cohesion, capabilities and creativity and create a favorable environment in which CPC members will learn from advanced people, become one of them and finally outpace them.

After the 18th National Congress of the CPC, Xi Jinping also stated: "To follow the party's leadership firmly is the key to build a strong army, so we must unswervingly adhere to the party's absolute leadership over the army and follow the party's orders and instructions at all times and under all circumstances." He went on: "We must give priority to strengthening the army through ideological and political work in order to keep it politically correct and firm in its construction. We must consistently arm soldiers with the socialist theoretical system with Chinese characteristics, continue cultivating the core values of modern revolutionary soldiers and carry forward the army's glorious traditions and good conduct, which can further enhance the ideological and political foundation for soldiers to hold high the banner of socialism, follow the party's orders and fulfill their mission."[47] These are the essence of the lessons the army has learned from its past nearly 80 years' experience, and the fundamental guarantee for the army to stay focused on its goals and to overcome difficulties.

Modern countries are all led by one or more parties. Since the whole organizational system of the PRC is under the leadership of the CPC, the army, as part of the state apparatus, is surely under the party's leadership and acts in accordance with the law. According to China's Constitution, all power belongs to the people; the National People's Congress and the local people's congresses at various levels are the organs through which the people exercise state power. The system of the National People's Congress and the party system of multiparty cooperation and political consultation under the leadership of the CPC were all established under the CPC's leadership. The people must exercise state power, including military power, through the CPC's leadership and governance. Therefore the people's command over the army must be realized through the party's leadership, which is one aspect of socialist democracy.

---

[47] Xinhua News, http://news.xinhuanet.com/video/2012-12/05/c_124053150.htm.

Chapter 10

How Does the CPC Handle Its Relations with Other Countries' Political Parties?

As China's ruling party and the core and leader of China's political system, the CPC formulates the country's diplomatic strategies, guidelines, principles and policies. Therefore its aim of developing interparty relations is consistent with that of the government developing relations with other countries, though the government's diplomatic activities are not conducted in the name of the CPC. The CPC's interaction with parties of other countries is an integral component of China's overall diplomacy and has unique advantages and an irreplaceable position. The CPC attaches high importance to interparty relations and takes them as a significant part of its cause, a means to improve its ruling capabilities and an important approach to enhance its influence and international prestige.

I. The CPC's Principles and Policies for Interparty Relations

Sound principles are needed to fulfill the objective of establishing and developing party-to-party relations. Only when they are correct and obeyed by both sides can the goal of healthy interparty relations be achieved. Over years of interaction with other parties, the CPC has formulated its own set of principles and policies governing interparty relations.

The Third Plenary Session of the 11th Central Committee of the CPC convened in 1978 marked the beginning of China's reform and opening up and its socialist modernization construction. Having learned from the experience of the international communist movement, the CPC put forward the principles for establishing new interparty relations based on the international situation and features of the time. In September 1982, the 12th CPC National Congress formally put forward four principles governing the party's relations with communist parties of other countries and put them into the *Constitution of the CPC*. The four principles include independence, equality, mutual respect and non-interference in other parties' internal affairs. In October 1987, the 13th CPC National Congress applied the four principles to CPC relations with parties of all kinds. Though independent of each other, the four principles are closely connected, forming an organic whole of rich contents.

The principle of independence is the foundation for the new interparty relations. The CPC fully respects the independence of parties in other countries and honors their right to choose their own social system and development mode based on their national conditions; the CPC acknowledges their right to handle their internal affairs independently and to lay down their own guidelines, principles and policies based on their observation of their domestic and international situation.

The principle of equality is the key to building the new party-to-party relations. The CPC maintains that all parties, small or big, strong or weak, boasting a long history or not, in power or not, are equal. One should neither act as the leader of others nor should one order others around and impose one's opinions and behavior on them. Only when all parties are completely equal can their independence be assured.

The principle of mutual respect constitutes the prerequisite for building the new interparty relations. The CPC holds it as a natural fact that parties have different ideologies and modes of behavior because of their different experiences and present situations. Since the differences cannot be avoided, cooperation between parties should go beyond ideology. All parties should respect each other even though each has its weaknesses and mistakes. No party is superior or inferior to others. They can learn from others' lessons and achievements to improve themselves and enhance cooperation while reserving their differences. One should honor others' right to choose their own social system and development mode based on their national conditions and to handle their internal affairs independently.

The principle of non-interference in other parties' internal affairs provides the guarantee for developing the new party-to-party relations. The CPC maintains that one's internal affairs should be managed independently without any interference from other parties and that no party should intervene in other countries' state affairs through its party connections since such behavior hampers the establishment and development of state relations.

In addition, no party should act against a third party and jeopardize a third party's interests through its bilateral party relations. Nor should any party, via its party relations, export its ideology, values, social system and development mode to others. Instead one should leave others to decide on their party principles and policies.

Keeping abreast of the new development trend of party-to-party relations, the four principles above manifest the aspirations of parties all over the world for independence and peace, and embody the nature of new interparty relations. Moreover, keeping up with changes in the international situation and party politics, the principles are consistent with the Five Principles of Peaceful Coexistence and other widely acknowledged norms regarding international relations, therefore gaining increasing endorsement from political parties around the world. They have become the fundamental principles for the CPC to deal with political parties from other countries in the new era.

II. Goals and Objectives of the CPC's Interparty Relations

Only when common objectives are realized through interaction can the development of interparty relations and cooperation be guaranteed. For the purpose of advancing the human cause of peace and development, when interacting with other parties, the CPC adheres to the win-win concept and gives full consideration to other parties' demands while pursuing and defending its own interests, which manifests both its patriotism and internationalism.

The CPC always regards safeguarding world peace and stability as an important objective and a permanent aim while building and developing its interparty relations. Suffering from imperialists' repeated invasions in modern history, the Chinese people long for and cherish peace. During the time of revolution and war, the CPC's contacts with the Communist International (Comintern), the Communist Party of the Soviet Union and other advanced forces in the world were aimed at seeking the victory of China's revolution and victory in the world anti-fascist war, and to win peace in China and the world as a whole. Faced with the confrontation and intensification of the Cold War between the Capitalist bloc and the Socialist bloc after the founding of the PRC, the Chinese government put forward the Five Principles of Peaceful Coexistence for state relations in 1953, which include mutual respect for sovereignty and territorial integrity, mutual nonaggression, non-inference in each other's internal affairs, equality and mutual benefit and peaceful coexistence. These five principles, though directed at state relations, can also be applied to party-to-party relations. Since entering the 21st century, the international situation has been generally stable, yet regional wars happen from time to time and hot issues keep appearing. Under such circumstances, China holds high the banner of peace, development and win-win cooperation and unswervingly works towards safeguarding world peace and pursuing common development. Sticking to the spirit of equality and mutual trust, inclusion, mutual learning, win-win cooperation and the principles of fairness and justice in its international relations, the CPC has been, through its party connections, working towards promoting many peace-making negotiations between relevant parties, making a great contribution to world peace, regional stability and the building of a harmonious world of enduring peace and common prosperity.

The second goal of developing interparty relations is to promote state relations. The CPC contacts parties rather than governments, which means such interaction is not concerned with state affairs. But interparty relations help promote the building, development and consolidation of state relations. Shortly after its founding, the PRC established state diplomatic relations with the Soviet Union and other socialist countries in Eastern Europe and other regions and later with countries of different political systems thanks to its relations with the communist parties of these countries.

Later, due to serious divisions between the CPC and its Soviet Union counterpart, both being ruling parties, relations between the two countries were affected and eventually became split, which also took its toll on China's relations with some socialist countries in Eastern Europe. Since the reform and opening up, drawing on lessons from its past experience, the CPC has made a clear distinction between party relations and state relations, which is to make sure that the former helps to promote rather than disrupt the latter and to enhance friendships between people of different countries and relations between countries. Under the guidance of this principle, the CPC takes enhancing relations between China and other countries as an important aim and safeguarding the national interest and promoting state relations as its ultimate goal when conducting interparty interaction. At the same time, it avoids letting interparty relations get in the way of state relations or even replace it. Since the reform and opening up, the CPC's work on its international relations has played a positive role in improving China's relations, friendships and cooperation with other countries.

The third goal is to serve the reform and opening up and the socialist modernization drive. As China's ruling party, the CPC has the responsibility to safeguard the interests of the country and its people, and always takes realizing national prosperity and the renaissance of the Chinese nation as the aim of its work. With the launch of China's reform and opening up and the changes in China's diplomatic policies since the early 1980s, the main goal of the CPC's interparty interaction has been to create a favorable environment for China's economic development and to serve the reform and opening up and the socialist modernization drive. This goal is consistent with China's interests and meets the hopes of other countries' advanced parties and the trend of the time. Since the end of the Cold War, people all over the world have been asking for peace, stability, cooperation and development. All parties, whether in power or not, long for a peaceful international environment to develop their countries, especially those in the developing world where the needs of poverty-alleviation and economic growth are much more urgent. Therefore, this goal meets the aspirations of most parties in other countries, which manifests both the CPC's patriotism and internationalism.

III. The Content and Forms of the CPC's Interparty Relations

With an increasing number of parties and an enlarged domain of interparty relations, the CPC is expanding the content of its interparty interactions from mere politics to various fields including the economy, culture and society, and is enriching the forms of interaction.

Strengthening political dialogue through which opinions are exchanged is the main task of party-to-party relations since parties do not handle state affairs directly. Parties can introduce each other to their domestic situations and exchange ideas on international and regional issues, especially their opinions about their interparty relations and state relations, which can enhance their understanding about each other, their friendship and interparty cooperation. Since the reform and opening up, CPC leaders have joined the party's foreign delegation visits every year to meet state leaders and party leaders of countries that have visited, or will visit, China afterwards. CPC leaders also meet many foreign party delegations and state leaders in China. The party has established communication mechanisms with parties in Japan, Australia and other countries. By introducing their domestic situations and exchanging views on international and regional issues of common concern, political dialogue can help seek political consensus and common ground while reserving differences and promote mutual understanding and trust.

Exchanging ideas on party and state governance is one of the important goals of interparty relations. It helps improve the CPC's ruling capabilities by drawing on other parties' merits and lessons. At the same time, with the accelerated development of China's economy and its growing international status, an increasing number of parties from other countries hope to learn about the CPC's guidelines, policies and strategies for party and state governance. Through communicating ideas about state and party governance, the CPC can learn about other parties' important experiences in reforming governance methods, leadership systems, working mechanisms, ways of handling relations between the party and the people, and ways to adjust and expand the social foundation, which is to promote the party's innovations in theory and practices. At the same time, parties in other countries learn more about China and the CPC's ruling methods and draw on the CPC's experiences in state and party governance.

Keeping abreast of the trend of economic globalization, the CPC is adding the facilitation of economic and cultural cooperation to the important tasks of its interparty relations. In recent years, the CPC has intensified efforts to research and discuss other countries' economic and cultural developments by enhancing comprehensive interaction with parties in these countries so as to learn from each other. When CPC leaders go abroad on official visits, people from the economic, cultural and business fields are allowed to accompany them, which creates opportunities to communicate and cooperate with other countries in terms of the economy and culture. In addition, the CPC serves as a link for provinces and government departments to build economic and cultural connections with other countries by importing foreign investment, technology and talent, creating new forms and contents of its international interaction.

In recent years, CPC delegations have incorporated **study trips** into their foreign visits and have sent delegations specifically for study purposes with a wide range of interests. They learn about other countries' economic structural adjustments, economic projects, public servant system, administrative reform, judicial system, the building of a clean government, urban management and transportation systems, news and publishing industry, broadcasting, the television and movie industry, cultural development, education situation, public health and tourism industry. Apart from the above-mentioned general study contents, study groups with specific subjects are also sent abroad to compile reports to help relevant departments in their decision-making. Such forms of study help CPC cadres of various ranks to broaden their horizon and acquire all kinds of advanced knowledge and management methods, which plays a positive role in elevating the CPC's governance capabilities. In recent years, the party has received many parties from Asia, Africa, Latin America and some developed countries in response to their hope to learn more about China. The party allows these foreign delegations to visit both the coastal developed areas in eastern China and the western under-developed regions. Here, they learn about not only the situation of party building but also China's economy, society, education, culture and public health, which helps them get an overall picture of the country and the CPC's guidelines and policies.

The second session of the High-Level Sino-American Party Dialogue held in Washington, December 4, 2010 (Zhang Jun, Xinhua News Agency)

Holding seminars on theoretical issues with foreign parties is part of the content and form of the party's international activities. Changes in the international situation and world party politics pose many new theoretical problems for parties of all countries in terms of party building, national development, and international and bilateral relations, which motivates all parties to find solutions to these problems, share development experiences, seek theoretical consensus and promote common prosperity. Bilateral and multilateral seminars between the CPC and other parties, whether in power or not, discuss various topics including their national domestic issues, party issues, and international and regional problems. The international department of the CPC holds several seminars where the party and its counterparts in other countries discuss and exchange views on major world challenges. Such seminars where various opinions are exchanged about theoretical and real issues contribute to broadening horizons, expanding consensus, inspiring new ideas and promoting cooperation, and help drive parties to make theoretical innovations, strengthen their party building and deepen understanding and friendships between various parties.

In conclusion, party-to-party interaction plays a unique and positive role in promoting the establishment, development and consolidation of relations between China and other countries. Exchanges of experiences regarding party and state governance help improve the party's governance capabilities and promote the healthy development of world party politics. Adding economic contents into interparty relations serves China's reform and opening up, the socialist modernization construction and economic and trade cooperation with other countries. Exchanging views on problems of common concern deepens mutual understanding and trust between China and other countries, which contributes to world peace and stability. Publicizing China to other countries through party-to-party interaction shows the CPC's open attitude and its aim of working towards development and cooperation.

An Introduction to the International Department of the CPC

Under the leadership of the CPC Central Committee, the International Department is in charge of the CPC's foreign affairs. Its main responsibilities include implementing the CPC Central Committee's guidelines and policies on foreign affairs, keeping track of and researching changes in the international situation and major global problems so as to report to the Central Committee and suggest solutions, acting as the liaison between the CPC and foreign parties and political organizations, and coordinating and managing foreign affairs of the organizations directly under the Central Committee's leadership and CPC committees in all provinces, autonomous regions and directly-controlled municipalities in a centralized manner.

Since its founding in 1951, the International Department has been under the care and direct leadership of the Central Committee, expanding its scope of work by conducting international exchanges, serving the party's key tasks in different periods. In particular, since the Third Plenary Session of the 11th Central Committee of the CPC, the department has been based on the four principles of independence, equality, mutual respect and non-inference in each other's internal affairs, fully engaged in carrying out the party's overall policies on foreign affairs, deepening party-to-party exchanges and new types of cooperation. The purpose of this lies in deepening state relations, serving the reform and opening up and the socialist modernization drive as well as the state's overall diplomatic strategies, consolidating the party's ruling position and promoting the building of socialism with Chinese characteristics. The Department interacts not only with communist and left-wing parties around the world but also with national democratic parties in developing countries, politicians, international organizations and parties of different ideologies and natures including socialist parties, labor parties and conservative parties in developed countries. To date, the CPC has built relations with more than 400 parties and organizations from more than 140 countries, most of which are in power or participating in the management of state affairs. A new pattern of the CPC's international relations has been formed featuring all-round, multichannel, wide-scope and in-depth exchanges and cooperation, which can be described as 'making bosom friends around the world and finding kith and kin across oceans'.

Under the new circumstances, the International Department is committed to growing into a department focusing on the study of international problems with great domestic and international prestige and distinct characteristics in order to provide intelligence support to the Central Committee's diplomatic policy-making and its party and state governance. It serves as an important window for the party to get to know the world better, further understand it and reach out to it, strive to create a favorable international environment of peace and stability for China's development and further contribute to world peace, common prosperity and human advancement. (source: www.idcpc.org.cn)

Chapter Follow-up Questions and References

Chapter 1

Questions:

1. How to understand that the CPC is a Marxist political party with an advanced nature?
2. Why should China uphold the leadership of the CPC?

References:

1. *Constitution of the Communist Party of China* (Beijing: People's Publishing House, 2012)
2. Fan Ping, *A Course of Party Building in the New Period* (sixth edition) (Beijing: Central Party School Press, 2003)
3. Liu Jingbei, *On Handling Party Affairs and Party Discipline* (Shanghai: Oriental Publishing Center of China Publishing Group Corp, 2014)

Chapter 2

Questions:

1. Why is the multiparty cooperation and consultation system under the leadership of the CPC a historical inevitability?
2. What are the unique advantages of the multiparty cooperation and consultation system under the leadership of the CPC?

References:

1. Li Jinhe, *A Study on China's Politics and Political Parties* (Beijing: Central Compilation & Translation Press, February 2007)
2. Lin Shangli, *The Communist Party of China and National Construction* (Tianjin: Tianjin People's Publishing House, January 2009)

Chapter 3

Questions:

1. What is the CPC's organizational system?
2. How do you understand the CPC's organizational system?
3. Why should we uphold the principle that the party should supervise its own conduct and run itself with strict discipline?

References:

1. *Constitution of the Communist Party of China* (Beijing: People's Publishing House, 2012)
2. Publicity Department of the CPC Central Committee. *Important Speeches by General Secretary Xi Jinping* (Beijing: Xuexi Publishing House, People's Publishing House, 2014)
3. The National Steering Committee for Cadre Training Materials. *Make Party Building More Scientific* (Beijing: People's Publishing House, Party Building Books Publishing House, 2015)

Chapter 4

Questions:

1. How do you understand the governance experience of the CPC?
2. How do you understand the governing methods of the CPC?

References:

1. *Decision of the Central Committee of the CPC on Strengthening and Improving the Building of the Party Style* (Beijing: People's Publishing House, 2004)
2. *Decision of the CPC Central Committee on Major Issues of Strengthening and Improving Party Building under the New Circumstances* (Beijing: People's Publishing House, 2009)
3. Yao Huan, *A Course Book for Party Cadres on Building the Party's Governing Ability* (Beijing: People's Publishing House, 2005)

Chapter 5

Questions:

1. How do you understand the tenure system of CPC congress delegates?
2. How do you understand the inner connections between the mass line and the intra-party democracy of the CPC?

References:

1. *Decision of the CPC Central Committee on Major Issues on Strengthening and Improving Party Building under the New Circumstances* (Beijing: People's Publishing House, 2009)
2. *The National Editorial and Steering Committee for Cadre Education and Training Materials, Development of Democracy at Grassroots Level* (Beijing: People's Publishing House, 2011)

Chapter 6

Questions:

1. How can CPC members demonstrate their vanguard nature?
2. How does the CPC give full play to CPC members' exemplary and vanguard role?

References:

1. *Constitution of the Communist Party of China* (Beijing: People's Publishing House, 2012)
2. Xi Jieren, *Construction of the Vanguard Nature of the Communist Party of China* (Beijing: People's Publishing House, 2012)
3. Liu Jingbei, *On the Building and Governing of the Communist Party of China* (Shanghai: Oriental Publishing Center of the China Publishing Group, 2014)

Chapter 7

Questions:

1. What do you think of the CPC's work in combating corruption and building a clean government?
2. How can power be controlled through established mechanisms?
3. How can the internet influence China's anti-corruption efforts? How can China integrate online anti-corruption efforts into its legal system?

References:

1. Hu Jintao, *Firmly March on the Path of Socialism with Chinese Characteristics and Strive to Build a Moderately Prosperous Society in all Respects – Report to the 18th National Congress of the CPC*, (Beijing: People's Publishing House, 2012)

2. The CPC Central Commission for Discipline Inspection and CPC Party Literature Research Office, *A compilation of Selected Remarks by Xi Jinping on the Fight against Corruption and the Construction of a Clean CPC*, (Beijing: Central Party Literature Press, China Fangzheng Publishing House, 2015)

Chapter 8

Questions:

1. Why is the united front an important instrument for the CPC?
2. How does the CPC correctly handle its relationships with trade unions, the Communist Youth League and women's federation?

References:

1. David Shambaugh: *China's Communist Party: Atrophy & Adaptation* (Beijing: Central Compilation & Translation Press, 2011)
2. China United Front Theory Research Association and the United Front Theory Research Center in Shanghai: *United Front Theory and Practice Frontier* (Shanghai: Fudan University Press, 2015)
3. Wang Ming: *Social Organization and Social Governance* (Beijing: Social Sciences Academic Press, 2014)

Chapter 9

Questions:

1. How did the PRC's military forces come into being?
2. What is your opinion about the leadership system of the PRC's military forces?

References:

1. The Information Office of the State Council of the PRC: *The Diversified Employment of China's Armed Forces* (Beijing, People's Publishing House, April 2013)
2. Wang Yiping: *Dreams and Goals of Strengthening the Army: Consolidating National Defense and Building Up the Army* (Beijing: The PLA National Defense University Press, October 2013)

Chapter 10

Questions:

1. What is the basic principle of the CPC's international relations?

2. What's your opinion about relations between the CPC and parties in other countries?

References:

1. Wang Jiarui and Ai Ping: *90 Years of the CPC's International Relations* (Beijing: the World Press, 2013)
2. Xu Yuemei: *Theoretical Studies of the CPC's International Relations Since the Founding of the PRC* (Beijing: China Social Sciences Press, 2003)